MAKE IT COUNT

Toolkit for Maximizing Your Life

Dr. Jake Oergel

Make It Count

Cover design by Carrie Doyle

Dr. Jake Oergel
Visit my website at www.drjakeoergel.com

Printed in the United States of America

First Printing: May 2019
Amazon Publishing

ISBN-9781726770682

First Edition

Dedication

The "Make It Count" Mission is, first and foremost, dedicated to my incredible family. It is also dedicated to those amazing individuals who live each day to the fullest; those individuals that take life's ups and downs in stride and make the most of every situation. Shall you never stop giving it your all -- because there are people watching, people taking notice, and people using your energy for betterment of their life.

This book is written in memory of my wife's cousin, Jimmy, who was the initial inspiration behind "Make It Count" as he battled brain cancer. Likewise, it is written to honor my best friend's dad, Mike, who lived the "Make It Count" mission every single day. He made everyone around him a success through his passion for life, until cancer won. Finally, it is written for my wife's father, whom I never had the privilege to meet. Though he lost his battle to cancer, his teachings raised a family of individuals who continue to crush life's goals on a daily basis.

Inspiration comes in many different forms. While the thoughts in this book spans a lifetime of experience. The creative aspect couldn't have been achieved without the atmosphere of my favorite coffee shop. Thanks, Mimi, for not only a place to think creatively but for also providing me with the world's best cup of coffee to fuel the process.

MAKE IT COUNT - Table of Contents   Page

Introduction

Words have the power to push us to achieve great accomplishments. How many times have you watched a movie, where you felt inspired by the main character's speech? How many times have you heard a quote, and then gone on to brand it as your life's mantra? The words you use throughout the day are the musings of your subconscious; our thoughts and actions are born from those words.

I remember the first time that the words "Make It Count" came out of my mouth. It was a difficult time, when a family member was dealing with brain cancer. My commitment to always wanting to make sure everyone in my circle is taken care of drove me to start a blog. The blog's focus was on driving belief patterns of making the most out of our days as nothing about tomorrow is guaranteed. A terminal cancer diagnosis drives many emotions into your mind; some thoughts geared at the "why me," while others focus on living for the moment.

Shouldn't we all live our lives with this same sort of emotional drive? Why not approach our days with the mindset that we have a limited time on this planet? Especially when the reality is that at the end of the day, we do. Time is a commodity that we can't ever make more of.

The blog evolved from a simple concept -- of wanting to make sure a family member rejoiced in the days' opportunities, to a beautiful application of "Make It Count." The mantra is geared at reminding us that each action has a reaction. If we approach everything with the idea that each experience is a new chapter, a new painting, a new approach to make a difference in this world, then everything we do will have intentions in giving you the life you have dreamed about.

Growing up, we are taught very structured ideas in school. Through all courses, we grow via conceptual thinking. However, what we don't learn, is how to truly live a life worth living. Success is rarely taught in a classroom setting, but more in the conversations, the attempts, the failures, and putting yourself in situations that test your comfort level. When we live a "Make It Count" life, we are constantly inspired to grow a little bit each day. Consistent growth ups our odds of making a substantial impact on the world. This, then, allows us to leave a legacy that we can be proud of.

There is no age requirement to apply these principles to our lives. The earlier we start in life, the earlier we have a chance to be the vessel of change we see ourselves becoming. I wish I would have been introduced to these principles earlier in my life. There's a common question asked to individuals who have accomplished a lot in their lives. They are constantly asked, "What is one thing you wish you could say to a younger version of yourself?" That question is the exact idea of what it means to live a "Make It Count" life. It's taking principles that we have learned through adulthood, through our own successes and failures, and through years of interviewing and studying other game changers. From there, the goal is to break down those principles into simple, applicable tasks that we can all take and apply to our daily lives. There is nothing more fragile in life then wanting, wishing, and hoping for change, only to consistently use the excuse of someday. "Make It Count" is about squashing the word "someday" and, instead, using the word, NOW!!!

Make It Count Forward: Susan Falkenhan

A roller coaster ride can be both exhilarating and terrifying. The ups and downs can produce incredible highs and distressing lows…much like life. Every day we experience moments of happiness, pangs of anxiety, and paralyzing fear of the unknown. This constant unpredictability often leaves one with a feeling that life is off center or out of control.

There is a way to regain balance to create a contented life, a life in which we can embrace the precious moments and deal with antagonizing setbacks. It requires a learned focus on what really matters.

Dr. Jake gets it. He understands the fleeting euphoria and agonizing defeat of life. He recognizes the demand of time and the relentless wave of emotions that batter our core. He has experienced life's emotional pitfalls, and he has worked relentlessly to develop ways to help navigate the fluctuations.

"Make It Count" doesn't eliminate the ups and downs and the uncertainty in life but acknowledges them and provides a strategy for better understanding how to live well. Dr. Jake delivers impactful quotes that can be zingers for thought, and he nudges us to break through what may be holding us back from a life of serenity and purpose.

The ultimate goal is to embrace each moment in your life and "Make It Count!" You are in charge of what you do every day and of how you react to moments in your life. If you fail, it is on you. If you succeed, it is because of you.

Food for thought: A rollercoaster with no ups and downs, twists and turns, is a flat line.

CHAPTER 1

The Juice Is Worth the Squeeze

"If you do what you've always done, you'll get what you've always gotten."

-Tony Robbins

The hardest part of life's journey is understanding what is worth your time, and what is not. Every potential situation comes with *three integral stages.*

The **first** is the thought: Will this be worth my time? The **second** is the action: The difficult part of putting pen to paper and pulling the trigger. The **third** is the reward: The stage we want the most but are sometimes not willing to endure the first two stages to get there.

This book was a thought for years. The idea stirred in my subconscious before my conscious mind decided to put the idea into motion. The motion was the most difficult part, mainly because of my thoughts, "What if I fail? What if no one likes the book? What if the principles contained with the 'Make It Count' lifestyle make sense in my head but are hard for anyone else from which to construct meaning?" All of these ideas gave me a daily reason to procrastinate. The excuses became my badge or identity on a daily basis.

It felt great to say I was writing a book like I had always dreamed of, but in reality, I was having the worst writer's block when I started. The excuses made perfect sense in my mind, and I could still say I was going to write a book. Then, one day while sitting three feet from the ocean on a peaceful vacation escape, I decided enough was enough and I started to write. The flow was easy -- the process took shape and with the simple action to start, I became what I wanted to be: an author!

It was never easy. The self-doubt was tremendous and the desire to quit never stopped. Does any of this sound familiar to you in your day-to-day quest? Times when you have a desire or a need, but the weight of the negative mind tries to steer you away from the path you desire? You start to build steam in your head. Will the journey be worth it? You gravitate to a fixed mindset of, "I don't have what it takes to fulfill that legacy."

Well, part of the "Make It Count" process is to tell you that the beauty in all of this is that the "juice is worth the squeeze." When you cut a lemon, you learn that the process is actually pretty easy. If the knife is sharp, similar to your approach or plan in life, then the knife glides through the lemon with ease. So the foundation of everything comes with having strong principles or paradigms in place. This foundation is your sharp knife. When you approach your goal, day, or life with precision, then the process is made easier. Go into battle with a rusty knife, no plan, or a lack of principle-based thinking, then everything will be made more difficult. Who wants to make things more difficult?

The most difficult step is always "the squeeze." You have to bring a determined amount of energy to the situation, in order to get the juice out of the lemon. However, once again, that amount of energy comes from your foundation. Your training, prep, and quest for personal improvement will have you ready for that lemon.

When I was a kid, my mom worked her 9 to 5 as a single mother supporting three kids. Her juice didn't stop as she regularly brought my sisters and I along for her 2nd, 3rd and 4th jobs. Her process never ended, but for her, the "juice was worth the squeeze." She was laying a foundational path for us, which taught us that taking care of your family should come first: you will always figure out how to get by in life when you put family first. She also taught us the value of hard work. Cleaning banquet halls became fun! My sisters and I turned what could have been a nuisance in our fun schedule, into our own adventure.

The amount of juice we can squeeze out of the lemon of life, is equivalent to the choices we make in everything we do. We can choose not to be present, to complain, to close our eyes to value, or we can look at every experience as a chance to grow.

I have spent the better part of the last twenty years chasing the Ironman Triathlon dream. The most difficult moments were not the races themselves. They were the endless laps in the pool - the thousands of miles done with my thoughts. They were the numerous injuries determined to throw me off the path. The only thing that kept me going through the peaks and valleys of training was knowing that everything I was doing was "worth the squeeze." All the time away from family was showing them what it meant to be committed to a dream. The grueling miles done at the track allowed the last few miles, after 9 hours of racing, seem like gliding through the air with ease.

Hard work sucks 100% of the time! Anyone who says they love every second of hard work has probably never really taken a step back and analysed why they love the hard work. The love affair does not typically happen during the moments of action, but rather in the results of the hard work. Workouts will suck, meetings will suck, sales pitches will suck, and some of the days will suck too! It's the reward of "the suck" that makes everything "worth the squeeze."

Without ever really pushing yourself to the brink of exhaustion, you'll never truly understand what you are capable of. Tears, cuts, bruises, failures, challenges to your confidence, other people's opinions, and the constant personal battle of **WHY**, are the "Willy Wonka Golden Ticket" to the journey of life. Michael Jordan would never have been "MJ," without a challenge in high school. As a sophomore he was cut from the varsity team. He set out that year to work harder then he ever did. He knew that all the extra practice would be "worth the squeeze." Tom Brady wouldn't have had a chip on his shoulder if he had been drafted in the first round. He knew that he would have to work harder than any other quarterback in order to prove himself and to prove that it was all "worth the squeeze". Tim Ferriss wouldn't have become the persistent lifestyle entrepreneur that he is, if *The 4-Hour Workweek* had been accepted by a publisher on the

1st go around – instead of being rejected dozens of times. Tony Robbins wouldn't have become the self-improvement guru that he is today without having had a challenging, abusive upbringing.

"The squeeze" allows us to capture the beauty of life in the framework of consistent hard work. It allows us not to just meet our goals, but to *crush* our goals. The process has to be a consistent and continuous battle to reconstruct what success means to you each day. Any great challenge is worth the difficult road if we know that with the first step, everything will be worth it in the end.

The last integral stage of the journey is the reward. This stage shows us that the journey is worth the effort. The reward can be as mighty as monetary gain, and as slight as putting a smile on someone's face. Either way, the reward is what lets you know that "the juice is worth the squeeze".

A couple of years ago, I spent about 6 months sending out two "Thank You" cards per day, to people I have come into contact with throughout my life. Some of them I didn't even put my name. The goal was just to let people know that someone cared about their path in life. The reward for me was in reminding myself that we all matter -- seeing people post on social media, about how a simple "Thank You" could inspire them to pursue their own goals in life.

Now is the time for *you* to embark on the "Make It Count" journey. You will learn how to educate, teach, and inspire others to be better, do more, and grow -- knowing that no matter how hard times get, life is "worth the squeeze!"

Make It Count Foundations

1. What is something difficult that you have recently been struggling with?

2. What have you accomplished recently that was worth the effort?

3. Which of the three stages have you learned from "the squeeze" that you can apply today?

4. List three things you can help someone with today to strengthen their "squeeze."

5. Life will challenge you around every corner. The goal is not to shy away from those challenges, but to take them head on. The goal is to realize that, while failure may be a result, the only true and final result is **GROWTH!!!**

Make It Counter: Gary Helmick

CrossFit Level 1 & Level II Certified
Bachelor's degree in Sport Management from Towson University

Gary Helmick owns (and trains at) CrossFit ReVamped in Columbia, Maryland. Since 2011, he has dedicated himself to learning about the Sport of Fitness. Prior to CrossFit, Gary was a student athlete at Towson University where he became an All-American short-stop. After his college baseball career, Gary played with the Baltimore Orioles organization for two years.

"CrossFit has simply become a lifestyle for me. Being a former elite athlete, I have been through many strength and conditioning programs over the years. None of these compare to what CrossFit has done for me physically, mentally and spiritually. CrossFit has woken a part of me that I didn't know existed, giving me amazing results and revamping my performance gains and competitive edge again. CrossFit continuously keeps me on my toes and that's what I love about it. The CrossFit community is such a fun, motivating, and hard-working group of people. I strive to inspire my gym and help teach the Sport of Fitness to the people of the community."

Some of Gary's accomplishments include:

CrossFit ReVamped Games Team 2017
Fittest in Maryland 2016
27th Place in the World at the Reebok CrossFit Games in 2016
5th Place at the Atlantic Regional 2016 which qualified him for the CrossFit Games
5th Place in the 2016 CrossFit Open Mid-Atlantic Region
2nd Place in the 2014 CrossFit Open Mid-Atlantic Region
38th Place in the World at the Reebok CrossFit Games in Carson, CA in 2013
2nd Place at the 2013 Mid Atlantic Regional
5th Place in the 2013 Mid Atlantic CrossFit Open
1st Place at the Winter Warmer 2013
133rd Place in the 2012 CrossFit Open
4th Place at the SuperFit Games 2012
All American short-stop at Towson University in 2009

Strength and Conditioning Athlete of the Year at Towson University in 2009
Athlete of the Year at Towson University in 2009
Former minor league infielder with the Baltimore Orioles
Bachelor of Science Degree in sports management from Towson University
PROGENEX Sponsored Athlete
FitAID Sponsored Athlete
Territory Sponsored Athlete

What are your top three habits?

My top three habits would consist of fitness, faith and family. I spend the most of my time revolving around fitness, one because it is my career and also because I have a passion for it. Faith plays a major role in my life. I live my faith through my faith and try to be the person God intended me to be. My family is my support system and I am always striving to be there for them as they are for me.

You have been very successful professionally, yet you are one of the humblest people I know. How do you remain so humble?

I think one of the reasons I can remain humble through my successes is because I hold myself to high expectations. With these high expectations, it makes me more modest because I already expect myself to accomplish a given task. Therefore, if the moment happens, I am not inclined to act proud or overbearing. I was also raised to always treat others how you want to be treated. It was ingrained in me to show class, sportsmanship and respect. I think being humble goes hand in hand with those characteristics.

What is the biggest lesson you learned while competing on the world's biggest stage in Crossfit?

I learned that there are some amazing human beings on this earth. There will always be someone out there that is better than me and that's okay. As long as I am working hard and staying true to myself and God, I am content.

You have developed an incredible community that transcends CrossFit. What is the secret?

I think the secret lies within some of my answers to the previous questions. I try to treat people with respect and pass along the qualities I've learned from mentors in my life. When I can display my most positive attributes, I think it rubs off on others and makes them better, which then makes our community better. People come to Revamped for fitness but at the end of the day, we all want an experience. We try our best to make sure their experience is one that will last and for that to happen, you must truly care about each other.

You have competed at the top level as a professional baseball player, and also as one of the Top 40 Fittest People in the world at the CrossFit Games. What type of mindset does it take to pull off such incredible achievements?

Both sports have some similarities when it comes to mentality. Like many sports, the real challenge is between the ears. With baseball you have to be a confident person. Mindset and approach is everything in the sport. It is an extremely technical sport that consists of a lot of failure. You must be able to deal with that failure in order to succeed. If you succeed 3 times out of 10 at the plate, you're doing something great. That also means you have to be okay with failing 70% of the time.

Crossfit is also very mentally demanding in many ways. There is the obvious level of suffering you must be willing to put yourself through. Then you also have the battle within on whether you gave it everything you had or not. This mental battle occurs just about every workout and some days you go home feeling like you achieved greatness and the next day will leave you pondering your abilities. Along with that comes the willpower to live an extremely healthy lifestyle. This comes in the form of food choices, alcohol consumption, sleeping habits and many more. All in all, the mindset you carry is a very powerful thing in whatever it is you're doing.

Two years in a row, you struggled to make it to the Crossfit Games due to injuries. How were you able to stay focused and not quit?

Like I said before, my faith and family were a huge part of my recovery and trip back to the Crossfit Games. I quickly accepted that I was injured, and I was never quick to anger or resentment in any way. I believed there was a reason for being injured and one of those reasons was to make me stronger in my faith. I also believed that getting injured may have humbled me as well. I do know the focus came mostly from the challenge itself: making it back to the Games. The fire was fueled within and I wanted to prove to myself that I could overcome the adversity.

What do the words "Make It Count" mean to you?

To me, Make It Count means living your life with a purpose. Be thankful for the day you have been given and try to live by example.

CHAPTER 2

Add Value – Deposits Vs. Withdrawals

*"You will get all you want in life, if you help
enough other people get what they want."*

- Zig Ziglar

Have you ever noticed how much better we feel when we tell someone, 'thank you?' Or when we give someone a compliment they weren't expecting?

There is an immediate and definite increase in our conscious energy. We feel better, we think better, we behave better, and we pursue our goals with more clarity. Our confidence increases, our passion grows, our mission comes into focus, and we trust that everything is 'gonna be okay.'

So, why is it that we consistently fall back into the trap of taking out a withdrawal once the hype of the deposit disappears?

The withdrawal is when we take value away from someone else; when we critique without intent to improve. We offer opinions based on self-serving needs, we talk behind someone's back, we joke about someone in front of others — knowing that the outcome will not build up their character. Most importantly, a withdrawal takes energy away from us and everyone involved.

There are 86,400 seconds in a day!

Imagine that someone gave you $86,400, and they said that you had to spend all of the money in one day. You cannot carry any money over to tomorrow and whatever is left will vanish. You could spend it on yourself — mom, dad, neighbors, or anyone you please — but nothing carries over, and the next day it resets to $86,400. What would you do in this scenario?

Sure, a new car, a fancy watch, or maybe an exotic trip would be incredible. But at what point would these selfish material objects lose their appeal? What if you took that money — that energy, that passion — and deposited it into other people's lives? Think of how great it would feel to be constantly doing good for others.

Well guess what? You CAN!

You don't need some big amount of money each day in order to do good. You have 86,400 seconds to give your full attention to those in your circle and beyond. Making deposits into another's journey allows us to inspire them to make game changing decisions in their own journey. The benefit to adding value to others is that you can watch your circle grow.

There is an old saying that goes, "you are the average of the five people you spend the most time with." So, if we add value to others we can ensure that the five people we associate the most with are authentic. These are the people that will help us to excel in this life.

Yes, I said *help* us to excel. That is the joy of making deposits. Zig Ziglar knew exactly what he was talking about when he said, "You will get all you want in life, if you help enough other people get what they want." The flaw in this thinking — because I can see some of your wheels turning already — is that if you intentionally set out to do good deeds with the expectation of something in return, you will indeed fail. There will be nothing authentic in how you approach your deposits. People are not stupid; they will be able to see through your Ponzi scheme. Plus, you have already set yourself up for disappointment when you don't get anything in return.

The goal is to start the day with the simple mindset of "I will do good, I will build trust, and I will improve the confidence of those I come in contact with." This, done with consistency and the intention of shaping a new lifestyle will come from a level of authenticity. That authenticity will morph itself into you becoming the person you wish to become.

People will see this when they interact with you — they will see someone who listens and disperses knowledge based on a growth mindset. They will know that you come from a place of striving for improvement. They will know that your passion lies in helping and caring. In turn, you will be rewarded with watching others grow towards reaching their dreams. The pure joy of watching others grow leaves a legacy in your journey of happiness. That legacy will be that you were a person that truly cared about others.

There will be a time, though, when you hit a low. And guess what? All these people you have helped with simple gestures along the way will be the first people to step up and offer their hands of assistance.

The genius behind "The Seven Habits of Highly Successful People", Stephen Covey, called this process the "emotional bank account." His paradigm was based on a level of trust. If we keep the emotional bank account with another person in a constant state of growth, then we can develop a lifelong trust with them. The second we start taking out withdrawals via discord, mistrust, broken promises, and words spoken behind their back, then the emotional bank account dips into the red. That bank account tends to close more quickly than we expect. But the great thing about emotional bank account is that we can salvage them when things don't go as planned.

Key ways to salvage an emotional bank account that has gone south include:

1. **Understand the difference** - We all respond differently to certain stimuli, to emotional triggers, and to alternative ways to regain strength. When we understand how a person is different, then we can learn how to attend to that person's needs.

2. **Simplicity** - One of the easiest ways to fix a situation — to realign with a forward direction and to start fresh — is to not overthink the situation. Never make things more complicated than they are. People, diets, communication, fitness,

writing a book, and the joy of life all form part of what should be simple. When we start over thinking our steps, we tend to make the wrong move or avoid starting altogether.

3. **Commitment** - If you are committed to fixing a situation, then go all in. If you told someone you would be there, then hold yourself accountable and show up. Commit to being better and, in exchange, you will get the respect necessary to grow any emotional bank account.

4. **Authenticity** - People are not idiots! If you are trying to mend a broken emotional bank account but it comes across as selfish, self-driven, or inauthentic, then you will never see a difference. Truly caring about another individual allows the situation to grow in confidence. Like a tree, they spread their roots for future strength.

5. **Admittance** - We all reach a point where we do something or say something unintentionally. Be the bigger person in every situation and admit when you are wrong. Even if it seems like an insignificant mistake or misjudgement, being the first person to admit wrongdoing allows your presence to grow as someone who has integrity.

In the end, the more you can deposit into someone else's life, the better it is for everyone involved. No one likes to end their day feeling empty, and I guarantee that no one likes to feel as though they've taken energy away from someone else's day. Be the bigger person every day and develop a "Make It Count" mindset — of helping, caring, and going the extra step — to make sure that those around you feel like celebrities.

Make It Count Foundations

1. How do you feel when you help someone? What is stopping you from doing it more often to get that immediate and positive conscious feedback?

2. What are three things you can do today to add value to someone else's life?

3. Write down how you felt when someone took a "withdrawal" from you. Did it build up confidence in your system?

4. Has your emotional bank account been empty lately? If so, what is one thing that you can do to change that?

5. Each morning make a list of how you will spend the 86,400 seconds you are given. Having a roadmap for your time will allow you to consistently add more value -- not just to yourself, but to everyone whose path you cross.

Make It Counter: Julie Reisler

Julie is a Doctor of Potentiality. Author and Life Designer®, Julie Reisler is the founder and CEO of Empowered Living, a Life Design and personal development company. Julie is a multiple time TEDx speaker, the host of The You-est You® podcast, and a meditation teacher on the popular app, Insight Timer. Julie has a master's degree in health & wellness coaching (with a concentration in nutrition), and more than twelve certifications in leadership, health, and well-being. Julie runs a coaching program, Monetize Your Purpose, for change makers, entrepreneurs, and coaches, and is the author of the Get a Phd in YOU book series (the companion journal to this book.) She is also the creator of the documentary and audio course on Insight Timer, Hungry for More. Julie is on the faculty at Georgetown University in their coaching program and is a Lululemon Ambassador. She is passionate about helping you master your inner world so you can crush it at work and beyond. To learn more about Julie, go to juliereisler.com

Your podcast 'The You-est You' is a "must-listen" among thousands of people. How did you go about perfecting the art of asking better questions?

GREAT question! Really, my intention is to highlight human beings who have moved through the common human emotions of fear, doubt, being stuck, frustrated, or not feeling good enough to a place of transformation and being able to live purposeful lives that serve the highest good of all. I like to ask questions that dig into that person's life, struggles and bumps in the road, but also their wins, growth and transformation. I have a background in coaching and appreciative inquiry which is all about asking open ended questions that get you to look at life from an appreciative lens. That training has certainly helped me.

You have written a best-selling book called Get a PhD in YOU I can't recommend the book enough but how do you think someone who lives The You-est You mantra would attend to a lifestyle of "Make It Count?"

Get a PhD in YOU is about going deeper to uncover your potential, move through old stories that have become roadblocks and become aligned with your sacred purpose. Being the 'you-est you' is about living into your highest aspect of yourself and making every moment count. Living your 'you-est you' is all about living a lifestyle that embodies the

Make It Count concept, as it's about maximizing each moment to learn, grow, serve and make a difference, i.e. to make it count both personally and for others.

If you only had 2 hours in the day to perfect your craft, what would you do?

The first thing I'd do, no question, is to set at least 30 minutes for meditation, gratitude journaling (what I also call intuitive writing), stretching and light movement and reviewing my vision board and life declarations. This routine sets me up to be as connected to my highest self and intuition as possible and to be clear and rooted in my way of being. I'd spend an hour reading articles or books about personal development, growth and mind/body wellbeing. I'd save the last 30 minutes to process what I'd learned with a trusted mentor, coach or friend, ending with notes from my call and an action plan how to implement what I'd learned. I actually try and do this most days, often with a lot of 'reading' done listening to podcasts, books and educational videos while driving.

What is the most difficult decision you have had to make in life?

The first would be deciding to end my first marriage with two little children under 5. This decision of listening to my intuition and moving on also led to my later decision to leave my corporate day job and start my own business. Both of these were about being my 'me-est me' and living authentically and according to my inner guidance and truth.

What is one piece of advice you would give a younger version of yourself?

Always listen to and trust your gut, as it will never steer you wrong. All is well and working out beautifully no matter how it looks or feels.

You travel all over the country, giving keynote speeches and inspiring thousands. What keeps you inspired along the journey? Where does your passion come from?

I have done so much transformation in my own life, spending thousands of hours on personal development, working with coaches, mentors, guides, being in support groups and even therapy. I have seen what's possible when you realize that you are worthy, sacred beings full of potential that can change the world for the good. Once I really got this at a cellular level - after struggling with a food addiction, thyroid autoimmune disease, getting divorced, going back to school for my master's degree, and leaving a stable and cushy job to start my own business...and changing my life through powerful coaching, I can't not do what I'm doing. In other words, there isn't a day I wake up where I'm not lit up and eager to make as much of a difference as possible. I would love to help and guide as many people as humanly possible to live a life that is full of self-worth, wellbeing, abundance and purpose. I have been blessed to be able to design my life in this way and hope to guide others to do the same. I believe we are all meant to thrive, experience inner peace and be joyful.

What are your 3 non-negotiables in life?

To be loving (to myself, and all others), to be kind and humble and have integrity (I think that's 4)

You have shared the stage as a motivational speaker with some of the biggest names in the business. What is a common theme you hear from these great minds?

Give more value than others expect, be authentic, care about whom you are speaking to and serving, be of service and speak from the heart.

CHAPTER 3

Sunny and Cloudy

"Whatever the mind can conceive and believe it can achieve."

- Napoleon Hill

There are many facets of life that we often overlook, ignore, take for granted, or neglect to self-evaluate. One of the most important parts of maximizing your day, is knowing how to take a second to actively express gratitude. We can all get incredibly busy (according to our own standards of busy), as we hustle and bustle down the path of life each day. Before we know it, we're going through our day on autopilot; self-programmed to perform the same tasks, over and over again.

Life will always throw hurdles your way. Your autopilot will either stumble along, or completely avoid the obstacle and go around it. Ryan Holliday's incredible book, "The Obstacle Is The Way," delivers the stoic philosophy of embracing obstacles in life and (more importantly) embracing our path as we go. Obstacles tend to be life's greatest teacher. Most people will see an obstacle and flee from lack of courage, lack of a plan, or a deep seeded "cannot-fail" mentality. The successful person doesn't see anything of an obstacle, but instead sees an opportunity to be better. They see the obstacle as a chance to solve a problem that needs to be solved.

We gloat over generations of successful entrepreneurs, but these amazing individuals didn't do anything special that the ordinary person couldn't do. They simply saw a problem and persisted in finding a solution. That solution became Apple, Uber, AirBnb, Instagram, and thousands of other companies that we rely on daily.

In life, we all come across days that end up being sunny, and others that end up being cloudy. In the end, mother nature decides how the day will turn out and this is not in our control. For years, I would stress over the weather when racing Ironman Triathlons, only to eventually realize that my energy was being wasted. I had no control over what mother nature would produce on race day. What I did have control over, was how I handled those sunny and cloudy days. My reaction was fully within my control.

The same goes for your perceived evaluation of "sunny and cloudy" interactions throughout your day. There is gratitude in sunny and cloudy events, as both allow us to understand the principles of life at play. When my kids were young, we started playing "sunny/cloudy" while seated at the dinner table each night. The game consisted of telling one thing that went very well (the sunny), and one thing that didn't go so well (the cloudy) during our day. This ended up being a vocal version of our "Five Minute Journal."

"The Five Minute Journal" involves taking a few minutes in the morning, to strategize your day and what you expect to go well. Then it is a few minutes in the evening, discussing what went well and how you could improve upon it the next day. Our "sunny/cloudy" was no different, in the sense that it allowed all of us to communicate how the "Make It Count" path went on that particular day in time.

The "sunny" allows us to see the good in life. It allowed us to see how we are adding value to others' emotional bank accounts. This could be as simple as, "I smiled more today than I have in awhile," "I helped the neighbor mow the yard," or "a classmate came up and told me how much they value our friendship." The goal is to personally evaluate the good and be grateful for what we have; to communicate, out loud, that life is about the experiences. This consistent evaluation of your day, shows that there is good in a lot of the things that we do. Sure, we might have had a pretty rough day. But that doesn't mean that we can't end the day with gratitude, and a simple conquest of what's "sunny" in our lives.

While the "sunny" consistently let my kids know that there was always good in the day, the discussions of the "cloudy" were what really made a significant impact on their growth mindset.

Initially, it was difficult for us to come up with "cloudies" to share with the group. In today's world, it's almost seen as weak if we admit to failures in our day. That way of thinking is so flawed, as having those "cloudies" is an avenue for growth. Humans, by nature, seek out the bad in situations. But we tend to harness those emotions internally, and we do not share as it might expose our weakness. Our family dinners halted at times, with too much overthinking of "cloudies" for the day — when, really, the intention of sharing a "cloudy" is to focus on a moment in your day that could have been better.

What didn't go well, and could have been improved upon? What action did you take that you know was not authentic to you? When we have this daily awareness, we are always in a learning state on how to become better versions of ourselves. This is where the 1% daily improvement paradigm comes from. Some of these *clouds* are not huge, life-altering decisions, but they are decisions that allow us to become 1% better each day when we use them for our personal growth.

Excuses are the gold within one's day. We hang our hat on excuses, as they give us a hall pass as to why things are *not* our fault. We have all heard the sayings before: "I didn't make the team because the coach doesn't like me," "I didn't have a good race because the weather was bad," "I didn't get a good grade because of the teacher," "I didn't get the promotion because my boss didn't notice the extra effort that I was giving." The "cloudy" discussion allows us time to talk out loud the event, excuse, action, or reasoning. This communication piece allows us, and those present, to investigate an event; to learn the parameters of what happened, and to create an opportunity to come out of the situation on the growth climb. The activity allows us to squash our excuses and open up about what we can do better in the future — to take more ownership in our lives. Plus, who better to talk through life's obstacles with than the people who love you the most?

There is no sugar coating as this environment is for growth and not lateral advancement. The talking it out allows you to realize that maybe you didn't make the team, not because the coach didn't like you, but because you avoided the extra practice all summer long. You realize that your place in the race wasn't because of the weather but because you skipped a bunch of crucial runs leading up to the race. You realize that the teacher had nothing to do with your grade, as they were truly there for help, but you decided to skip many assignments because your social media account was on fire. Finally, you realize that while you *have* been putting in a little extra work at the office, you are still constantly late, you rarely speak up in meetings, leave ten minutes early each day, and constantly ask for time off.

Practicing "sunny/cloudy" on a daily basis opens you up to so much potential in your life. It allows you to cancel the autopilot and be present. When we are engaged in our day, we can be in a constant state of flowing gratitude. The state in which you see, feel, and know the good happening all around you. This energy is contagious and it is what builds upon the "Make It Count" mindset. Each and every situation has a good and a bad. This is what makes us strong: knowing that the good and the bad are both steps in our path to the mountaintop.

Make It Count Foundations

1. What are three "sunnies" for your day today? How can you implement more "sunny" into your life?
2. What are three "cloudies" for your day today? What can you learn from them?
3. Who will you share the "sunny/cloudy" activity with today?
4. What is the purpose of being 1% better each day?
5. How will you cancel your autopilot today and be more attentive to your actions and surroundings?

Make It Counter: Suzy Serpico

My name is Suzy McCulloch Serpico, and am 38 years young. I started doing triathlons when I was in high school (1997) and never looked back. When I started, I would have never imagined how triathlons would influence my life. Through triathlons, I have been able to race all over the world at all different distances and meet so many new people. A few years ago, I stepped out of my comfort zone and made the jump to race professionally. I figured you only live once, so why not? I got to race with the best of the best and truly learn a great deal about myself. Currently, I have shifted from racing triathlons to what I call "participating". For me, it's not about beating the clock or winning, instead it is about pushing my limits and finding something that excites and scares me at the same time. I have participated in two Ultra Triathlons and absolutely fell in love. My new challenge for 2019 is the EPIC 5: five Ironmans in five days.

When I am not training, I get to share my passion of fitness in many other ways. I have been an elementary school Physical Education teacher for 17 years. My husband, Danny Serpico, and I own a race production company called Rip It Events. Along with that, I am head coach for Rip It Coaching and have coached many athletes to achieve their dreams.

What is your definition of success?

I think success is all defined upon the person. To be successful is not only being good at what you do but, more importantly, being happy in what you do.

You have competed at every stage of triathlon as a professional. Over the last 2 years, you have taken your experience to the next level with UltraMan Triathlon. You even recently broke your personal best by two hours and were first overall female. Explain what UltraMan is and what you learned about yourself through that experience?

UltraMan is a 3 day endurance race. Day one is a 6-mile swim followed by a 94-mile bike ride, day two is 171-mile bike ride, and day three is a 52-mile run. For me I have been doing triathlon for 20 years. I have completed over 15 Ironmans and I knew I was ready for a new challenge when the question was not IF I was going to finish but how well I was going to. Ironman still excited me, but I needed to find something that was going to excite me and scare me at the same time. Honestly, doing the Ultra allowed to me to renew my love for the sport. Too much emphasis was placed on winning and I began to not enjoy the sport. This year, 32 athletes from around the world participated. The Ultra World has taught me to really race against and within myself and instead of racing the people next to me, I was supporting them.

What is the most difficult decision you have had to make in your life?

Probably not what you are expecting but the decision to not have kids. It took awhile for me to be sure because society thinks you should get married and then have kids. However, I get a lot of satisfaction from teaching, coaching, and from being an aunt that I don't feel like I am missing out on anything.

Your energy and passion levels are always a 10 out of 10. What is your secret to never letting yourself fall below that metric?

I love what I do! I truly love helping people of all ages achieve something that they never thought possible. Whether that is helping a child make a basket or someone complete an Ironman, I thrive and get my energy from that. I am truly lucky to be able to share my passion.

From a teacher and professional athlete perspective. What piece of advice would you give someone in high school?

Don't be afraid to be you. There will be people who like you and people that don't in the world, and that's ok. BE HAPPY with who you are inside and out and the rest will fall into place. My high school quote was "there is no tougher judge than yourself" and I still believe that is true 20 years later

If you could put a saying on a billboard what would it say and why?

A saying that I have tattooed on my wrist and my family says before all my races…. REMEMBER WHO LOVES YOU. It is a saying that I have with my mom, dad, and sister and live by it every day. It is a saying that has taught me about unconditional love. I was, and am still not, the perfect child but no matter what, my parents showed me that it is ok to make mistakes and that family is forever.

If you wrote a book on the life of Suzy Serpico what would the title be?

Trust me I have thought about writing a book many times. I am not sure that many people realize that I have had my fair share of struggles physically, emotionally and mentally. I think people assume that since I am "fast" that I have it all together. I think the book would have to be "Can't Judge a Triathlete by their Results".

What do the words "Make It Count" mean to you?

You only live once so make this crazy life that we live worth it!

CHAPTER 4

Be Humble

"True humility is not thinking less of yourself but thinking about yourself less."

- C.S. Lewis

Have you ever heard the saying, "Actions speak louder than words?" In my 42 years of life experiences, interacting with all types of people, the most common single trait amongst these "game changers" has been their level of humbleness. Every single one of the contributors in this book has crushed life so far. Yet if you were to sit down with them for a cup of coffee, you would never know their level of success, because gloating is not a growth habit of successful people. Each of these individuals would be more interested in how *you* are doing, where *you* are in *your* chapter of life, and how they can help get *you* to where *you* need.

Does this sound like the definition of someone who is humble in their offerings? It sure does to me.

To be humble is to know that you are not perfect in anything that you do. We live in a world where movies, media, and books refer to the notion of "survival of the fittest." It is the idea that you must crush everything and everyone in your path and show no mercy. It implies that admitting weakness is a flaw, and that we must all wear a badge to show off our medals, our awards, and our resumé. However, the problem with this thinking is that many of these people often hit the ceiling and they don't know how to break through. They have taken the short cut to success, but they have learned nothing about themselves along the way. They have ignored their weaknesses, they have burnt bridges, and they have run for the hills in panic at the first sign of difficulty.

When we use a level of humbleness in our lives, we agree to the foundational elements of caring for others, increasing our ability to improve upon our weaknesses while cementing our strengths, and having a mindset that there is no level of failure which can't be broken through. Being humble allows us to engage in personal confrontation as though it could potentially be the greatest interaction of our life. We learn that no one is below us and no one is above us, but instead we are all on an equal playing field of mutual growth.

One of my good friends, Gary Helmick, is the epitome of what it means to be humble. In 2016, I had the absolute honor of coaching him and his wife to the Crossfit Games. The Crossfit Games are a culmination of the 80 fittest male and female athletes in the world. These athletes were whittled from thousands down to hundreds and then to the top 80 competitors. Those competitors then competed over 5 days, to be crowned the king and queen of the competition. Gary has qualified twice for these games, is a former professional baseball player, and owns one of the top Crossfit gyms in the country. However, his focus each day is on how he can make his community better. He focuses on which weaknesses are holding him back from being the best version of himself, and on how he can be a better husband to his wife. Not once, will you hear him brag about his accomplishments.

This personality trait is one that becomes contagious and it makes one naturally want to become a better version of oneself. The goal in each day should be to build our life's resumé full of incredible experiences. When we focus one day at a time and realize the potential of the "Make It Count" mentality, then the foundation laid by this book becomes an easily obtainable fabric of your conscious and subconscious decision making process. The experiences turn your mindset into a purpose driven machine. When that machine is churning out care for others, then everyone benefits.

The villain to being humble is the **ego**. We all have moments in our day when we love to take our ego for a spin. The dangerous part of this spin is that sometimes it feels good for all the wrong reasons. Our mind starts to focus on me, me, me, and "what can I do to help me?"

Personal accomplishments are exciting and fun, of course. We need to soak them in, while also harnessing their dark side. When we keep focused on *ourselves*, and think it is always about us, then we start to lose sight of the bigger picture. Our leadership fails, our happiness for others fades, our community turns, and it becomes a game of one. Eventually, we are on an island all alone.

To avoid the pitfalls of the "all about me" mindset, here are 5 principles of people who embrace the right mindset and know how important it is to be humble:

1. **Humble people display pure happiness for others.** People who are humble see others' beauty and are truly excited for others' accomplishments. We all grow when we can embrace the success in our triple C - circle, community and competitors.

2. **Humble people see weakness as the foundation of growth.** They don't ignore their strengths, they just know that repeated growth over time is the strongest activity we can pursue. It is internal reflection on what we can improve and then taking action on that growth which produces strong leadership.

3. **Humble people make exceptional leaders, as their community knows that they are authentic in their guidance.** Anybody who has followed a great leader knows, without doubt, how authentic that leader is. They wear their emotions on their sleeve, they have an open door policy, they promote open idea sharing amongst their staff and they are authentic in their mission.

4. **Humble people know that no matter what, everything will work out in the end.** Confidence in the journey ahead, comes from having a solid foundation.

When your paradigms, mission, metrics, and principles are in place, then your confidence grows. Having a "Make It Count" daily passion instills trust in all of your decisions — knowing that no matter what happens, success will be present.

5. **Humble people let their actions speak volumes.** It's easy to talk a big game. All it requires is for you to open your mouth and just keep spewing information. It really doesn't matter if it's true or not. Some people will see through the fog and others will believe everything that comes out of your mouth. Humble people know that the best form of education is through action. Talk is cheap, but actions educate the masses.

The last great notion of a humble individual, is that they are correctable. They love the idea of a "teach me" approach which they understand is needed to be successful. Someone who thinks they know it all can be difficult to interact with because they can't be corrected. They never admit to wrongdoing, wrong ideas, or wrong placement. It is always *someone else's* fault. When someone is humble, they are aware that they don't know everything. They are thirsty for knowledge. They are correctable in the sense that if there is a better version, they want to know that version ASAP and apply it to their foundational mission.

Make It Count Foundations

1. Do you consider yourself humble? If so, why?
2. What is one thing you could do to become more humble? Choose one pathway and start improving on that path today.
3. Identify your top three weaknesses and write out an action plan to attack those three weaknesses on a daily basis.
4. Learn to be open to being corrected. This has been my hardest "Make It Count" advancement point, personally. Being told a better way to do something has always hurt my personal philosophy, until I realized that it's not about me, but about the bigger journey/legacy.
5. Have a mindset of greatness. This allows you to open yourself up to the idea that things can always be better — no matter the situation, time, or surrounding community. Every situation has the ability to make us grow, and that growth is what the journey is all about.

Make It Counter: Julia Roman-Duval

I am Julia Roman-Duval. I was born in Normandie, France in 1982, and I am the oldest of 4 kids. My family traveled quite a bit as we were growing up. We lived in several cities in France, and I actually spent most of my childhood (age 10-17) in Reunion Island, a French island in the Indian Ocean. My parents raised us to be very athletic and outdoorsy. I have always spent most of the day outside playing, and that has not changed a bit! Alongside my husband of 11 years, Miguel, I am now raising our three children with the same lifestyle. Our favorite activities are outdoor playing, sports, hiking and other adventures (such as electric skateboarding, cliff jumping - we love the Beaverdam swim club!). We don't go a day without some good outdoor time, rain or shine, warm or cold. We also delve into exciting science topics on a daily basis, as both Miguel and I are scientists and are keen on sharing our passion with the kids.

From a young age, I have been passionate about math and physics, particularly astrophysics, the study of the Universe and how everything in it works. While my dad is a literature guy, he is somehow the one who gave me this passion. He is very methodical and taught me the reasoning process for solving problems during homework time. Solving math problems became a game and hobby. When I was about 10 years old, I read a science magazine (for kids) about special relativity. I got hooked and wanted to become an astrophysicist. Fortunately, I was successful in this challenging quest. I completed my PhD in Astrophysics in Boston in 2009 and I am now an astronomer at the Space Telescope Science Institute in Baltimore. I spend half my time pursuing my research about the interstellar medium (the nebulous gas and dust between stars) in nearby galaxies. I spend the other half of my work time supporting the Cosmic Origins Spectrograph (COS) onboard the Hubble Space Telescope. This entails a lot of calibration work to make sure the instrument always works optimally to serve the science community. My work as an astronomer is not just a job, it is a lifestyle, just like running.

I was into many, many sports in my childhood and early adulthood (even ballet) believe it or not I snuck out to the karate class next door and never went back... However for a long time, I could never find the one sport I really loved. This changed in my mid-twenties when I discovered triathlons, adventure racing, and other endurance sports. These sports fit my driven personality, keen on always pushing the limits. I trained 2-3 hours each day throughout grad-school and became one of the top triathletes in the North

East. After my kids were born however, and after nearly a decade of dedicated triathloning, it was time for a change of "career". I was exposed to and hooked on competitive running when I joined the Howard County Striders' racing team. I started training with them in late 2013 and they basically changed my life. I met my very best friends in this group. They inspired me and supported me to accomplish some great running achievements, such as qualifying for and going to the 2016 marathon olympic trials, amongst others. And we had some amazing laughs and comradery along the way.

What is your favorite quote and why?

I don't really have a favorite quote. I don't know many in fact. When I come across a quote, I enjoy pondering over whether or not it resonates with my own experience or sentiments (or the experience I see in other people). But quotes don't play any role in the path I choose for my life, or how I view the world, so I don't bother to remember them. Why? Because quotes are just words. The character of a person, their leadership, or moral principles are much better reflected by their actions. I have had several role models who inspired or guided me to a certain path with my life by the actions they took, not the words they spoke.

But if you ask, here are some of my favorites I have seen so far:

"You must do the things you think you cannot do" – **Eleanor Roosevelt**

"Life is like riding a bicycle. To keep your balance, you must keep moving" – **Albert Einstein**

"The bad news is time flies. The good news is you're the pilot" - **Michael Altshuler**

As a professional athlete and astrophysicist, you have already accomplished so much in life. What are your daily non-negotiables that help support your success?

You forgot the most important component of my busy life, my family! Juggling semi-professional running and my career as a scientist is part of my life's accomplishments, but what I am the proudest of is my husband and three children. Those three pillars of my life (family, work, running) are all an integral part of who I am. I pour all my energy into this lifestyle, and because those things make me happy, the energy pool seems to replenish itself constantly.

As for successfully juggling all family, work, and competitive running, a big part has to do with the support of my husband, Miguel. The other part is really wanting to succeed at all of those aspects without compromise. We have a good routine that works and also makes all of us happy and fulfilled; we rigorously stick with the plan and the schedule. Tired or not, whatever the weather, the alarm goes off at 5.30 am and I am up in a heartbeat, ready to go. I cannot go a day without some outside time and a good workout, either a hard one to push my limits, or an easy one to clear my head and enjoy the outdoors. Morning is the only time I can get it done, so that is the way we roll. At 4:30 pm, whether my daily work tasks are complete or not, I leave the office, because the kids and I need to spend some time playing together before we get to all the evening duties (homework, dinner, bath-time etc.). That's also a non-negotiable. I cannot go a day without playing and cuddling with Miguel and the kids. I get more work done after they're asleep, which means that I rarely get to bed before 10.30-11 pm. This is the last non-negotiable, since I have to get the work done to continue being successful in my career. I have wanted to pursue this career since I was ten-years-old and I could not possibly compromise it. I guess that means sleep is negotiable!

Keeping this kind of schedule everyday can be challenging and exhausting. It certainly is ambitious. Therefore, it is important to be receptive to the body and mind's feedback and the warning signs for burn-out. From experience, I cannot go at this pace for more than 3 months at a time without getting hurt (physically or mentally), at which point a vacation or "staycation" is absolutely necessary.

You have had some high level races over the past two years that have not gone well, but you seem to grow with strength, energy, and focus each time. What is your secret to having a strong growth mindset?

I have been like this for as long as I can remember. I must be wired this way, but the way my parents brought me up and my siblings probably contributes. I am the oldest of four children. Positivity was always the mindset at home: you grow from your mistakes and make the most of what you have. Throughout my early life, disappointments or "failures" (I don't think anything can truly be a failure, but they may be regarded as such from the outside) were temporary setbacks, obstacles in life that represent opportunities to learn, replenish one's motivation and determination to achieving a goal, or just staying on the path that one chooses. A concrete running-related example from one of my recent races: The Cherry Blossom 10-miler. I trained hard in the winter and early spring to get in shape and PR at that race. But on race day, I had nothing. My legs would not respond, I was stiff and had no energy. I was upset and angry at myself after the race for not being able to keep it together and execute the way I should have been able to given my level of training. After the temporary mental upset passed, I realized that I just did not have the willpower to go chase my goal. I needed to be frustrated with myself, I needed a good kick to get the adrenaline going and I needed to remind myself why I was waking up early every day to go out and run hard. A couple of weeks later, I was so fired up to make up for my last, disappointing race that I ran a personal best at Pike's Peek 10k, and again one week later at the Broad Street Run (10 miles). I was just so ready to go fight and race with all I had!

What piece of advice would you give a younger version of yourself?

Don't let others influence or dictate what you are capable of; don't let anybody break your confidence and determination. There were a few times in my life when I lost confidence in myself because of how others (more senior) people treated me or what they said to me. I entered the preparatory school system in France when I was 18. This is an elitist, competitive school system which crams a four-year math and physics curriculum in two years to prepare students for the competitive entrance exam to the French "Grandes Ecoles". This system nearly broke me, physically and emotionally, not only because of the immense pressure they put on the students, but also because of a couple of professors who were just plain mean and who abused their power. I am one of the lucky ones who went on to succeed, but I wish I had been stronger then and had not let them affect me or get through to me to the point they did.

What is your earliest memory of success?

I am trying to think back. I was about 8 or 9 years old. My elementary school used to take us to sports classes, which I always loved. They had us try a really wide range of activities, from trampoline to rock climbing or swimming, even horseback riding. We also had a few months of judo. I really enjoyed it. I was a tiny kid, short and skinny, but fairly solid (I was and felt stronger than I looked!). For my second fight, they paired me with a chunky boy, who was one year older and a full head taller. I was not intimidated (but then, I was fearless and hardly ever intimidated anyway). The coach had barely started the fight when I got the boy with a direct ippon which is a point in Judo for a perfectly executed technical move. Poor guy hit the mat before he could even register anything. As far as I can remember, this was the first time I felt I had really accomplished something. I was proud of myself for not getting intimidated, and for pushing myself physically.

You seem to be getting faster with age as a professional runner. What are your three secrets to success as a professional athlete?

I think it takes more than 3...

- Healthy diet
- Lots of strength work and cross-training, lots of maintenance (that includes my monthly visits to you)
- Sufficient sleep (I make sure I get my 7 hours most days, I may get 6 occasionally), and a longer night leading to Sunday (I sleep 9-11 hours that day)
- I set ambitious but achievable goals that I believe in. But I am not afraid to set the bar very high. Then I keep my eyes on the prize, always.
- I really try hard to work out a smart and efficient training plan to achieve said goals, and I stick with it, no matter what
- I always mentally prepare for hard workouts and races, working through the logistics and what will go on in my mind, what thoughts I will have to have to embrace the pain and succeed
- I am not afraid to push myself so hard physically and mentally that I am ready to collapse by the end (I have...).
- I have fast and supportive teammates to train with!

You have accomplished so much in life yet are so extremely humble. How does one stay humble while growing success in life?

Tough question. I think it is a personality trait first of all. But I can see how success can make a person less humble than they originally were. Indeed, as far as running is concerned, I am not quite as humble as I used to be to be honest. Perhaps that is due to my perceived increased level of confidence, which I have earned through hard work.

I don't have a good or clear answer to this question, but I have a few hints. I think I don't get satisfied, ever. I always need and want to push the limits, reach higher, further, keep chasing new goals. I don't rest on my laurels! I don't think that is compatible with not being humble.

I also am inspired by other people who accomplish great things, and I keep a down to earth big picture perspective on my/our role here on this planet. We are so minuscule in the grand scheme of things! I think we all have talent or drive in different things. When you respect someone for their character or what they have accomplished, you natural develop a humble approach. I really don't like to brag for this reason, who am I to say I am better than someone else!

What do the words "Make It Count" mean to you?

Our time here is limited, and one never knows when it will end; One should make the most of every second. The practical implications are that **1)** we should try to fulfill our dreams no matter what. **2)** we should not shy away from big goals, limits can be pushed. **3)** we should keep a positive mindset and see the good in people and in what happens in life. **4)** we should enjoy time with loved ones (family and friends). **5)** we should enjoy the simple things in life, such as going for walk or playing with family.

CHAPTER 5

Other People Focused

"Service to others is the rent you pay for your room here on earth."

- Muhammad Ali

Everything starts with a foundation, because without one nothing can be built to withstand the storms and battles that occur when we least expect them. The foundation of the "Make It Count" lifestyle will forever be ingrained in an "other people focused" mentality. Throughout life, we get wrapped up in so much personal drama that we typically start each day with a focus that life is all about the self. The reality is that when we flip the focus onto others, we live a complete life with the deepest success we can ever experience.

Your goal in life should be to live each day according to the type of funeral you would like to have. Do you want a funeral based on a quick service, attended by only a couple, obligated family members? One that lacks stories and an absence of your legacy? Or would you want a funeral that is standing room only, in which the energy is palpable? One that celebrates a life full of meaning, in which a legacy was left for generations to learn from?

A couple of years ago, after crushing life for 96 incredible years, my wife's grandmother passed away. At her funeral, even those who had never met her could have walked away with an appreciation for the life she lived. After the formal service, we stayed for about 2 hours, crammed into the small church. Without hesitation, people stood up to share their numerous stories on how this amazing woman had touched their lives.

They told stories of an unrelenting commitment to build a better community, daily. They told stories of the love, care, and passion that this woman had for life. They told stories of gratitude: of how this one, single person had changed their perspectives on how they would attack their own personal journeys. There were dozens of stories of unselfishness — how this lady had put her personal agenda aside in order to be a sounding platform for personal growth. Most importantly, they told the stories of a 96-year-old woman who lived the "Make It Count" lifestyle every day of her life. She did so by constructing a belief that every person she came into contact with did have a special purpose in this world.

When we are "other people" focused, we ignore and eventually lose the negative traits we've developed over our lifetime. We stop talking behind others' backs, we stop thinking of our personal agenda first, we develop communities based on the growth of everyone involved, we inherit a deep gratitude for being happy for other people's successes, and we listen with the intent to help other people. Being "other people" focused stops our monkey mind from destroying conversations that may have a lifetime of impact.

How often in a conversation do you truly listen? My guess is that well below 25% of the time do we actively engage in listening during a conversation. We are typically thinking of our response or interrupting with a response before the other person is done talking, or maybe day dreaming about what the rest of our day will look like.

Next time you're in a conversation, try to really focus hard on the person you are communicating with. Listening is not an easy feat. Your mind will naturally gravitate towards only partially listening, and partially trying to formulate a quick response. Listening is an extremely difficult skill that takes lots of practice and a deep care for the other person's advancement. Human nature is to want to be selfish and to wonder what is in it for *us* and *only us*. We tend to care just about our own growth, and we invest so much energy into our own opinions that we short change the conversations we have. We don't want to be open to what others have to teach us, because it might go against what our foundation says. In the long run though, growth is a two-way street.

Being "other people" focused is not saying that we need to agree with everyone. It is the belief that other people's views sometimes *need* to be heard, and that when they are heard, there can then be a meaningful conversation that helps everyone grow. Here is a tip for the next time you sit down with someone and engage in conversation: Try to listen with the intent to help. When they are done talking, and only when they are done, take a couple of seconds to come up with your response. This will give both of you the respect that you deserve. It will give the conversation more depth, as you are taking the time to think of an authentic response. And I guarantee you will walk away a better person for investing that time in an efficient manner.

Remember that old coach you had -- the one who always seemed to be on your back? The one who was constantly hounding you for not doing the right thing or for messing up on a repetition? For me, that was a football coach from my freshman year of high school. He was one of the toughest coaches, teachers, mentors, and leaders that I had ever trained under. There wasn't a day that we didn't run more, that we didn't do more burpees, or that we weren't told how we weren't "good enough" and that we were "all slackers with no future." We never lost a game, but there were days we dreaded knowing that in a mere few hours we would be crushed by our coach once again.

It's been about 30 years since then, but I still can't stop thinking about what his goal was. He never said that we had to win, he never mentioned getting scholarships, and he never talked about the stats. What he *did* mention were character, respect, team, encouragement, perseverance, appreciation, gratitude, growth, strength, leadership, values, metrics, love, sacrifice, and always being better than we were yesterday. He pushed us hard, not because he was a terrible coach, but because he cared deeply about us, and wanted us to invest in ourselves. Great coaches put aside their personal agenda and they know that their position has to inspire a movement of change. They know that when their foundation of being "other people" focused is working in an efficient manner, their team will grow as a unit. And when teams grow as a unit, everyone wins.

To live a "Make It Count" life, we must commit to helping others. When we make this commitment, we expand our network to inspire future success. When a community bonds around being "other people" focused, there is no confusion over what the mission of everyone involved becomes. When we live an "other people" focused lifestyle, we will never be alone in our journey. Life will get hard, I guarantee it. But when our circle is strong, others won't hesitate to help us in our time of need.

Make It Count Foundations

1. What are three things you have done this week that have been "other people" focused? *(If you're having trouble with this answer then the next question would be: What three things will you implement today to be more "other people" focused?)*

2. What type of funeral do you want to have? What do you want people to say at your funeral?

3. Do you consider yourself a good listener? How will you improve this communication skill moving forward?

4. What mentor, coach, colleague, or classmate can you think of who has lived an "other people" focused lifestyle?

5. *Life* is about *living*. What principles do you think you could incorporate into your life, that would help you become a better, more "other people" focused influencer?

Make It Counter: Peter O'Dunne

Peter O'Dunne is a small business owner and commonly refers to his role at Mid-Atlantic Rubber Company as the "Culture Keeper." He is passionate about leadership in all aspects of life and is an author of a book called *From Rust to Trust*, about the success and happiness of living by principles in business, while training and competing for the Ironman competition. Peter is a certified facilitator of "The 7 Habits of Highly Effective People" and has facilitated 25 classes over the past 15 years. Peter is most proud of his role as a father to an amazing daughter and of his role as loving husband for 33 wonderful years.

What book have you gifted the most in your life?

From Rust to Trust -- yes, it's my book and I wrote it to share with others. I have gifted hundreds of signed copies to friends as well as complete strangers. I can say now that it really does feel better to give than to receive. I have so enjoyed surprising people that I meet with my book and workbook. I recently got a thank you card that included the following quote by Bob Kerrey: "Unexpected kindness is the most powerful, least costly, and most underrated agent of human change."

You have written a successful book on the story of your life called From Rust to Trust. What does "From Rust to Trust" mean? What did you learn about yourself during the process?

"From Rust to Trust" defines the many journeys that happen to each of us many times throughout the year. I like to divide these journeys into those that we decide to create ourselves and those journeys that just happen to us. I choose to train and compete in the Lake Placid Ironman annually. And each year I begin in a pretty rusty state and by the time I hit the start line, I am prepared and confident about the race. Friends of mine choose to lose weight, or quit smoking or hundreds of other planned journeys that will take them from point A to point B. The other kinds of journeys are the ones that happen to us such as a sickness, financial crisis, etc. The two types of journeys are similar in that to be successful, they must both begin with a vision and a plan to move from Point A to Point B. We are all dependent (rusty) when we are in a new role or experience, but we must quickly move on to becoming independent and eventually interdependent (trust). Independent people take responsibility for their lives, show initiative, and don't blame others for their circumstances. Independent people have goals and purpose in their lives. They get results and accomplish meaningful things. It takes two independent people to become interdependent. Interdependence is where principle-centered and other-focused people hang out and trust is the hallmark of interdependent people.

If you could give a piece of advice to a younger version of yourself what would it be?

I think it would be to figure out what everyone else is doing and do the opposite. This mindset works at any age and I think where it works the best is in designing the life that you want to live. It's going back to the idea of a vision. Creating a vision of what you want your life to be like is huge. It's huge because part of that vision creation is to become self-aware; to begin to notice what your true God-given gifts and talents are, what your passions are and what they are not. Life can be so fulfilling when you are living life by design.

What one thing has had the biggest impact on your life?

Creating a personal mission statement. I was in my mid-thirties and really struggling with life balance and life's purpose. I remember going on a business trip to Florida and staying two extra days with the idea of detecting my personal mission. This was not my idea but from Stephen Covey. Thirty years later, I still live by that mission statement. The quality of my life and my relationships is directly linked to the fulfillment of my mission.

You have completed close to 20 Ironman Triathlons over your lifetime. Your most recent have been over the age of 60. What is your secret to the fountain of youth? Most people slow down later in life, and yet you seem to be picking up steam.

I am still living my mission to "inspire others by...." and I am inspired by those that continue to compete. I joke that I got into Ironman competitions because as I aged, it was taking me longer and longer to warm up. Hence, I needed longer events. The truth is that I heard someone say that what you do in your sixties will determine how you will live in your eighties. I try (tri) to do some form of exercise 6 days a week and I try (tri) to always be in half-ironman conditioning. I also have a new "purpose" to raise money for my wife's cancer. Racing with the TEAM for CURES helps me to do that and it is a win-win for everyone.

You have studied under Stephen Covey who wrote *The 7 Habits of Highly Successful People*. What is the top lesson you learned that you still apply today?

I have learned so much from *The 7 Habits of Highly Effective People* and I can say that single program changed my life forever. The term that Covey uses, "effective", refers to trusting relationships. Unless we are living on an island in seclusion, who does not want to have all their relationships be "trusting relationships?" So first, I would encourage anyone to attend this 3-day course. The take away for me is habit #5 "Think Win-Win". This habit encompasses the two paradigms in life that I follow: Being principle-centered and being other-focused. People think they know what it means to think Win-Win but they often don't. Thinking Win-Win means that you listen, really listen to figure out what a win is for the other person before you think about what a win is for you. Our human nature is just the opposite: to think about ourselves first and then the other person. And most of us are not very good listeners. When done correctly, the end result is amazing and usually ends up with a solution that is better than either party could have developed on their own. If I was teaching this habit "Think Win-Win" in a class, I would reference the movie Lion King. The two paradigms in the Lion King best teach what win-win is and what it is not. Under the rule of Mufasa, Pride Rock was thriving, and everyone followed a paradigm of "Abundance". There was plenty for everyone. When Mufasa was killed and replaced by Scar, the paradigm shifted to "scarcity" (Scar), everyone for themselves, no sharing, just survival for the fittest. Of course, the "Abundance" paradigm best defines win-win and the "scarcity" paradigm defines win-lose, lose-win, or lose-lose.

What are your top three non-negotiables in life?

To be faithful in my marriage, to always be a leader worth following by staying positive and optimistic, by treating others how I would like to be treated and never stop trying to improve.

What do the words "Make It Count" mean to you?

If it's worth doing, it's worth doing right. Life is really short so making it count means not to waste time on things that are not important. The important things are your key relationships which includes the relationship you have with yourself. Detecting and living by your mission will help to keep you focused, especially as the unexpected occurs. You will make better decisions and have better relationships. You will be living life interdependently which is a "win-win" for all.

CHAPTER 6

Write Your Story

"There comes a point in your life when you need to stop reading other people's books and write your own."

- Albert Einstein

How will you be remembered? What impact will you make? What mark will you leave? What will people learn from you? What will your legacy be? In the end, all of these questions will be answered in a story told by someone other than yourself. But you still have the ability to influence what goes into that story.

Your legacy will follow how others thought of you — whether that's near the end of your time at a job or coming to the end of crushing your goals on this planet. We can't tell people exactly what it is that we want them to say about us, but we can live a principle driven life aimed at laying our foundation in others minds. When we live according to the "write your own story" principle, we focus on a few simple paradigms geared toward forming a legacy to last for generations. Writing our own story allows us to constantly be focused on what we are doing. The key is to remember that what we say and do are actually who we are.

The mistake is usually when we say what we are. This often becomes a projection of what we *want* to be, and it's rare that we actually follow through on those thoughts. For example, if I say that I live *every* day to its fullest potential or that I try and see *everything* with an optimistic view, it is a projection of how I *want* to live my life. This is what I preach, and this is how a "Make It Count" lifestyle is lived. But maybe in reality, my actions are in contradiction to this — consistently late to meetings, talking behind others' backs, not following through on commitments, promising more than I can deliver, always complaining how things are not fair and generally having a negative outlook on life's situations. You can see the contradiction in the two approaches. One is a shiny outlook on my ideal life, and the other is the harsh reality of my actual life. Which will be remembered more? The talk or the action?

One action we can take is the simple art of writing. Writing and journaling have allowed me to establish a truce with my monkey mind. That is, the wandering mind that can't stabilize consistency in thoughts. It's the mind that runs from thought to thought, with no plan. It's the mind that generates genius ideas, and also the mind that is destructive in its growth patterns. When we physically put pen to paper, we get those great ideas out of our head and into reality. We can develop lists, pros and cons, next step ideas, and a pattern for a life we would like to live. Great ideas die early when not put into action, and negative thoughts grow in possibility when we hold on to them for too long. Another problem when we don't write our own story is that we often get trapped into just going through the motions.

When we only go through the motions then not only does our story lose its excitement and benefit to others, but our story becomes boring to ourselves. When we live to just exist, then there are no defining moments that leave a life worth remembering. Having purpose to writing your story allows you to embrace everything that happens during the process. Tracking your days and how you become 1% better creates a pathway that enables you to identify whether what you are doing is leaving a mark within your community or not.

The whole goal of writing your story is to continually remind yourself that you are in charge of the ship. You are the captain of this journey. You are the person of influence in designing your "Make It Count" lifestyle. If you don't take the wheel on the ship, then you become just a shipmate and you live in accordance to someone else. Someone else is then in charge of telling you what to do, how to think, what steps to take, and how you should respond. Does this sound fun to you?

Not to me!

Having a process each day to make sure that you're telling your own story becomes a crucial part of any and all success in living the life you want by design. Journaling, writing, and typing can, and will, become an integral part of your growth. When we put those items down, they either disappear like they are intended to, or they grow because you are taking action to make something out of your thoughts. Passion comes from your own words and thoughts, and not from someone else. No one can give you the conviction to pursue your dreams, challenge your goals, and keep your head above water when times feel tough.

5 Strategies for Writing Your Own Story:

1. **Have a morning routine**. — Waking up early without distractions sets a tone for successful growth. This time allows you to set a foundation for your day's story that is consistent each day. It's a time when you can decide what you will do that day, how you will respond, and what your focus will be.

2. **Physically write down your thoughts.** — Taking the time to actually write down your thoughts builds a routine of growing positive ideas and dispersing negative ones. Spend 10 minutes just writing. Don't worry about grammar or sentence structure, just write whatever comes out. You will find a groove and you will know what your next step needs to be.

3. **Read what you write out loud.** — Reading what you wrote out loud allows you to know where your mind is. Are you in a fixed mindset, or growth mindset state? Are you on the verge of something great, or on the verge of a breakdown? Either way, the power of knowing your space can guide you in building the legacy you desire.

4. **Share your story.** — When we share our story — our principles, our desires, our dreams, our goals, and our wants — we develop an accountability with others. That makes us vulnerable, but when we share that vulnerability, we build confidence that we are on the right track.

5. **Revisit your story every night before bed.** — When we can sit back each night and review our day, we know how authentic we were to ourselves that day. Did we hold true to our principles? Did we follow our mission in life? Or did we choose a wrong path, so that tomorrow we must correct our course? This time allows us to always be on track with who we want to be.

In the end, the story is yours to be written. It can be one that focuses on yourself as the main character, or maybe as a supporting role. Either way, make sure that *your* choices are your choices. Keep evaluating your process and making sure that you are satisfied with the direction in which the ship is sailing. Don't be afraid of taking risks, as those risks might be part of the next chapter in your life's story.

Make It Count Foundations

1. Do you have a writing routine?
2. Are you satisfied with the story you have written so far?
3. What can you do, right now, to change the tone of your story?
4. Sharing your story is the most positive experience you can have. When we share, we learn from what has worked and what has not worked during our journey.
5. Remember that your story is *your* story. Never compare your "Chapter 1" to someone else's "Chapter 10." We are all on a different journey, so keep strong on your story and be your own author.

Make It Counter: Joanna Lohman

Joanna has been a professional athlete for fourteen years and is currently a midfielder for the Washington Spirit in the National Women's Soccer League. She has utilized her platform to impact people around the world. She is a human rights activist, a professional speaker for leading organizations and she also serves as a Sport Diplomat, traveling the world and running programs in less developed nations that promote gender equality, conflict resolution, cultural understanding, and economic development. She has helped individuals and groups find their cool by living an unabashedly authentic life based on deep-rooted acceptance and discovering comfort in their own skin. Joanna recently launched her own personal development program: "Defining Your Beauty." This amazing program can be found at joannalohman.teachable.com

What is the one piece of advice you would give a younger version of yourself?

It is cool to be vulnerable - to open yourself up to be totally present in the moment and to feel. Use those feelings to grow and build awareness of who you are and who you want to be. And do not be afraid to express those feelings through your passions.

Regardless of your personal journey there will be pain and moments of struggle. Do not numb those moments because you will get through them faster if you embrace the challenge. And always remember, you are beautiful and valuable. Love yourself unconditionally and know that no matter how hard it gets, you are not alone.

What is your favorite quote?

I have two:

"To give anything less than your best is to sacrifice the gift." - Steve Prefontaine

"The man who moves a mountain starts by carrying away small stones." -Confucius

You have succeeded at every level as a soccer player. What is the one common thread that you believe has consistently kept you at the top?

Resilience. Courage. Authenticity.

Ironically enough, I think what has kept me at the top is realizing we are ALL at the bottom. Together. And that I am only one part of a community that has empowered me with acceptance. Being at the bottom means we have to constantly learn, grow, and get better.

I want people to know that I have overcome a lot of challenges in my career with a fearless determination. I want them to know that I stood for something. Something greater than myself. I want them to see the effort I have put forth to grow the game and connect with the incredible fans we have associated with it.

I want people to know that I cared. I cared a lot. I cared about the game, I cared about my teammates, I cared about the sport, the league, the fans, and everything and everyone involved.

That I gave my all in every single practice, game and interaction with a fan. I gave my heart, body, mind and soul to the sport, to the growth of the game, and to my impact on it.

I want people to know I tried to make a difference, to make people feel SOMETHING - empowered, inspired, cared for, loved, accepted, included. And to know this by genuinely and honestly being unabashedly myself.

If you wrote a book about your life, what would the title be and why?

The Adventures of the Rainbow Warrior - it encompasses my entire life and what I stand for.

You have an incredible passion for life. Where does that passion stem from and how do you find the energy each day to keep that passion alive?

The passion stems from gratitude and responsibility.

The platform to impact another human being as a professional athlete is unparalleled. I want to use this platform to inspire and advocate for equality. I want to make every fan that attends a game feel like they belong to something special - the women's soccer community - and that their contribution is valuable. Sport has the power to change the world and I want to be a part of this positive change. I will use the stage to consistently strive for betterment. I also realize that my occupation is a gift. I get to do what 99.9999% of women around the world have zero opportunity to do. I am privileged and I view this privilege as a responsibility to stand for others who are unsafe to do so. I want to be a voice for so many who are forced into silence.

What is your earliest memory of success?

When I think about success, I think about the unconditional love my parents showed me throughout my entire life. The earliest memory is a story my mother told me.

When I was about 7 years old, I played my older brother in a game of tennis. I lost to him that day (and many days after). I was so upset because I hated losing. My mother watched from a hill next to the court. As we walked home together, I held my mother's hand in silence still fuming from the loss. My incredible mother knew no words would cheer me up. So, instead, she squeezed my hand that was interlocked with hers. In that subtle yet powerful gesture I knew she was telling me that she loved me and because of that love, everything would be okay. We walked a few more yards and I said out loud to her, "I love you too." I then ran off ahead with a smile on my face. This love my parents instilled in me consistently reinforced that regardless of any result, I was a success because I was worthy of love.

You suffered an ACL injury that could have ended your career. What did you learn through that process that has helped you to return even stronger?

I learned that ANY journey will be hard. Very hard. So it is important to take it one day at a time and ALWAYS have hope that it will get better - because it does - with time and dedicated work.

I took the time in the beginning of the injury to really process the sadness and let go of who I thought I "should" be that season/year. It's almost like you have to mourn the death of the pre-injury self (for the time being, obviously). Once you do that, you can truly embrace your REAL self EXACTLY for who you are in that moment - that takes a lot of weight off of your shoulders.

I promised myself that I would love my life for exactly how it was and not what it might be or what I wanted it to be. For instance, I tried to never say..."I can't wait to run", "I can't wait to be cleared", etc. because that dismissed the beauty of the present and the beauty of the struggle.

When I look back on my ACL injury, I say it is the best thing that has ever happened to me. I say that because it was hard as hell, but I made it through and I made it through with an attitude of love, gratitude, and appreciation for even the smallest victories. With this attitude, you can celebrate the tangible and intangible moments of physical, mental, emotional, and spiritual growth. There truly are SO MANY.

Also, I made sure to always remember I was NOT ALONE. There were so many people going through a similar struggle and so many friends, family, fans who were there to support me in my darkest and brightest moments. Do not be afraid to lean on them. Everyone is better for that.

What do the words "Make It Count" mean to you?

To me, those words mean that our life is a gift that enables us to uniquely contribute to this world. Our contribution is valuable and worthwhile. And, we must understand that every choice we make is a representation of the legacy we will leave on this world. Leave a legacy you are proud of.

CHAPTER 7

Dream Big but Wake Up

"Some people dream of success, while others wake up and work hard at it."

- Winston Churchill

Do you know what separates the *dreamers* from the *doers*?

Action!

Everyone, and I mean everyone, dreams on a daily basis of something they would like to achieve — a goal they have in their mind's eye or something that burns with passion deep inside their soul. The problem with these dreams is that they stay inside us, hidden from the world, never to see the light of the day. We visit those dreams, from time to time, but the visit ends very quietly, and life moves on. The greatest distracter of dreams is *life*. We often know what we need to do, in order to push the needle forward on our dreams, but we hesitate. The dreams are too risky, we have no experience, there will be a better time, it's too expensive, we'll be in better shape later, or maybe it might not work.

Have you ever heard the saying, "The road to success is always under construction?"

Life's plan will always get in the way so it's important to wake up and show results every day. When we don't take immediate action, we tend to get frustrated and take a negative route instead. When we consistently speak of a goal — a dream, or a visualization of something we want to accomplish — but we don't take immediate action, then we tend to get too frustrated to even take the first step. We talk a big game and get ourselves worked up over the possibilities, but we falter into a negative tone when action is not taken soon enough.

For years, my mentor wanted me to write a book. It's something I have always wanted to do. When I was in the fourth grade, I won our state's "Young Authors" competition with a book about the adventures of a tarantula, named Stanley. As a 9-year-old kid, the idea of taking a concept and putting it on paper to tell a story had me full of passion. It was as if Stanley, coursing through his adventures, was me on my own day-to-day adventures. I absolutely loved the idea of writing a book from start to finish.

Fast forward, over 30 years later, to when my mentor asked me to write a book. At first, that same joy and attention that I had at 9 years old, bubbled to the front. However, every day that I woke up and I didn't start by putting words down, was a day I grew more and more frustrated with the process. Each day that I didn't start became a day where I questioned all the "WHY'S" - why should I write a book, why do I think I could write a book, why would anyone read what I had to say and why spend all this valuable time telling my story. Each day that I didn't start put more of a negative tone in my mindset over the passion I had at 9 years old. I had the dream of creating this book that would leave a legacy for my kids, my family, and whomever took the time. But the dream started to get scattered with negative thoughts: "I can't write," "No one will read it," "It's too difficult," "What will I say?" and a plethora of other thoughts that were obstacles to keep me from starting.

Then one day, I woke up with that young passion I once had. I realized that the longer I took the route I was taking, the longer I would be following a path to nothing. That "nothing" was going to happen, unless I took the first step. That "nothing" was going to happen unless I made some forward momentum and started to make waves. In order for our dreams to become reality, there will have to be **sacrifices** made. Personally, I have to give in to the sacrifice of vulnerability because vulnerability comes with greatness.

The biggest gain you can make on your dreams is to decide that enough is enough; time is wasting and you do have what it takes. The world needs your dreams, and you need to WAKE UP! When you do, you will take that dream from the blank slate in your mind and you will introduce it to your circle. The dream, no matter what shape it's in at this point, has woken up. Congrats! This is the first step to success. Now you can hold yourself accountable which is needed for you to reach your final destination. Yes, the hard work and sacrifices will be difficult. But there is also fear knowing that your friends, family, and community are now aware of your dreams. This gives you the energy to stay up late, wake up early, and go the extra yard, knowing that you are now doing this for a bigger cause. It will be scary at first, but it's *supposed* to be scary; the things that scare us the most are also the things that challenge us the most. We can truly find what we are made of when we take these unknown steps into our new reality of dream chasing.

I am sure that when Jeff Bezos got started in his mom's garage, he had no idea that his world-domination-creation of Amazon would become what it is today. His brilliance is one part great idea, one part good timing, and one part turning his dream into a reality.

I have met numerous professional athletes who came from nothing. The one thing they each did was to open up their dream and work extremely hard making lots of sacrifices. When their friends were going out on a Friday night, they went to bed early — knowing that the Saturday morning session would be crucial to their future success. They sacrificed plenty, but only because they had a plan that involved putting their dream to work. I have interviewed, treated, and communicated with hundreds, if not thousands, of successful entrepreneurs. Some failed, while others succeeded. But no matter the result, everything was a win because they proceeded to chase their dream regardless of the path. They put their reality on the line and they went for it.

To some, Thomas Edison *failed* 1,000 times before he got the light bulb right. However, Thomas Edison would have told you that he *didn't* fail 1,000 times, but successfully learned 1,000 ways not to make a lightbulb. This positive thinking is only possible when we keep trying and pushing forward towards our dreams. When the dream sits in your thoughts, you never quite reach that one-time chance to see if it might actually work. JK Rowling knows this for she battled difficult times creating the magical world of Harry Potter. She faced having no money, being a single parent, being homeless, and working five long years to produce the first Harry Potter book. All that, only to be rejected by 12 publishers. But did she quit on her dream? You already know the answer to that question. She had dozens of chances to quit, but she never gave up on her dream. She fought daily to keep her dream alive, no matter the circumstances.

All examples of success are brought on by action, as action creates opportunity. Yet, opportunity is only available through action. Through waking up and creating momentum, the one thing we can't stop doing is dreaming. Dreaming allows us to use that imagination that was so powerful when were kids. Back then, our imaginations were the strongest tools we had. We believed we could be and do anything. One day, I was a professional basketball player. The next, I was a firefighter and the next, a surgeon saving the world. This kind of imagination broke down barriers, as it allowed us to think larger than life. It built confidence, kept our minds strong, and allowed us to continue to believe anything is possible.

As kids, we had no problem dreaming up a car washing business, a lemonade stand, or door-to-door sales. We saw all of our dreams as possibilities, and we acted on most of them no matter the outcome. At some point, reality told us that it wasn't ok to dream as big. It told us that it wasn't ok to have such a vast imagination, and that we needed to settle into a less risky lifestyle. I am here to tell you that the most powerful weapon you have is that imagination — and the dreams that come out of it. The "Make It Count" lifestyle believes that time is a limited commodity. Without actively chasing those dreams, we eventually fall into a life of regret. So dream big, wake up, take action, and fight like crazy to pursue the life you've always dreamed of!!!

Make It Count Foundations

1. What is the biggest dream you've ever had?

2. What is stopping you from pursuing your dreams?

3. Dreams become stuck in our thoughts when we don't take action in our lives. Write down three action plans you can implement today that will help you take action tomorrow.

4. We all have heroes, mentors, and people we look up to or admire. Who is this person for you? Interview this person or read about his or her life. I guarantee they didn't come from great beginnings, and that they had to fight for their dreams. Take notes on their story and try to implement some of the same fight into your day.

5. "Make It Count" is all about other-people-focused initiatives. What can you take away from this chapter that can help someone else to take action today?

Make It Counter: Aaron Magden

Aaron was literally born into the window business and started working in the warehouse for his father's window company in Cleveland when he was 14 years old. He learned the business from the ground-up, spending time in all roles from sales to management to operations. Now as the President of Window Nation, he works closely with his brother Harley building what's now the 5th largest home remodeling company in the US. Aaron created a unique sales system that revolutionized the industry, shying away from the typical "high-pressure" in home consultation. The Window Nation approach is customer-focused and designed to meet the needs of each individual homeowner first and foremost. Aaron leads the entire Window Nation sales operation across all offices in 7 metropolitan areas. A native of Cleveland and graduate of John Carroll University, Aaron now lives in Glenwood, MD with his wife and two girls. A die-hard fan of all teams in Ohio, he is particularly passionate about the Cavs and the Tribe and spends time working out when he's not at a game. *"Always provide a great product, with red-carpet service and a fair price."*

What does your perfect day look like?

- 8 solid hours of sleep
- Wake up early (6am) and workout. This allows for a productive day to come as this is my "Idea and Problem solving" time for the day. As I work out, I begin to think through the current challenges in work and life to solve.
- Family time. Spend at least 30 minutes with my two girls whether it be an activity or just helping them get ready for the day
- Eat a healthy breakfast
- At the office, greet everyone with a smile and a laugh to help my employees start off their days. Productive employees are KEY. If they aren't happy, they won't be productive.
- My workday as the president of Window Nation has evolved over the years from tactical day to day to a strategic leadership role. I'm the face of the company, which means people look to me for advice, leadership, and problem solving.
- My commute home is about 30 minutes which allows me to decompress before I see my family. This is the time when I contact family members and friends to see how their day was and exchange things that may have transpired that day, personal or professional.

- Eat a healthy dinner with my family.
- I travel quite a bit, so putting my kids to sleep is part of the perfect day.
- Spend time with my wife before bed. Anything from a conversation, to a TV show, or a date night.

Who has made the biggest impact on your life?

My father – in business and personally. He has helped shape who I am today. Having grown up in the home improvement industry, he taught me the business and created the relationships necessary to start Window Nation. Once he sold his company, which eventually led to the start of Window Nation, he provided the insight and support from our start to ensure success. Relationships are key, but nothing can replace hard work. He taught me what hard work was when I worked for him I never received special treatment as an employee. He always told me you have to earn your stripes just like everyone else and that there are no free meals in life.

My father's teachings were endless; Let me share a few:

1. He never let another man down. He fulfilled every obligation he ever undertook. His word was his bond, and everyone knew it. I never heard him utter a lie, nor intentionally deceive anyone.

2. He worked hard for a living, raising us as a single father since we were toddlers while building his business. Not an easy task by any means. But by doing that it instilled the hard work ethic we follow to this day.

3. He walked the talk. If he said he was going to do it, he did. He started his window company in the basement of his house, and everyone laughed at his picture in his ads with his thumbs up. The picture was taken with a camera no better than a Polaroid in his house and he put in in all his ads. He said watch boys, let everyone laugh. Pretty soon I'm going to put these guys out of business…. And that's what he did.

4. Breaking through barriers. He constantly reminded my brother and I how each Magden generation broke a barrier in business. His grandfather broke the first barrier coming over from Lithuania and started a produce business where he worked as a little boy. Then his father broke another barrier by starting a carpet business from scratch which at one time became one of the largest carpet companies in NE Ohio in the 70's. And our father broke the next barrier with

Regency Windows, creating the largest window retailer in NE Ohio and the famous Mikey character. And now my brother and I breaking the next barrier building the 5th largest window retailer in the country, Window Nation.

What has been your greatest failure in life and what did you learn about it?

- You hear so many quotes on failure and its importance to succeed which is 100% true. This is how we learn, from our mistakes and failures in life. To date, my biggest failure was the closing of our Charlotte location. But this failure led to many successes, the opening of 4 more locations since. I learned:
  - o **The Peter Principle**. This is an observation that the tendency in most organizational hierarchies, such as that of a corporation, is for every employee to rise in the hierarchy through promotion until they reach the levels of their respective incompetence. We promoted someone to open the branch as the sales manager that was above what he was able to achieve.
  - o **Oversight.** You gotta roll up your sleeves and be on the front lines when opening a new location. I trusted the manager in place which partially led to the demise.
  - o **Research.** Didn't complete the extensive research needed to understand the market wasn't a good fit. We ended up finding out the homes in the market were too new which led to less homes needing replacement products
  - o **Economy.** Charlotte was the banking epicenter and we entered at that time. Just a poor decision, but we pushed ourselves to grow.

What piece of advice would you give a younger version of yourself?

A goal without a plan is just a wish. Goals help us believe in ourselves. Setting goals for yourself is a way to fuel your ambition. Goal setting isn't just about creating a plan for your life and holding yourself accountable, it's also about giving us the inspiration necessary to aim for things we never thought possible.

Window Nation started with one client at a kitchen table over 12 years ago, and it has grown into a Top 5 specialty company in the country. What single action or focus has allowed Window Nation to keep growing year after year?

It's one of our core values: Never Settle. We instill this value in every employee that comes to work here. This means pushing you past your comfort zone, take daily action, and never settling for mediocrity. Everyone has KPI's (Key Performance Indicator) associated with their roles and we never settle for the benchmark. We pay hefty bonuses here rather than pay high salaries because we want our employees to push the envelope and attain the BIG goals we set out to achieve.

If you could only work 2 hours a day on Window Nation, what would you focus on?

Continued development of culture. Happy employees equal happy customers and I have a lot of influence in who works for us. Good people are hard to find, especially in a booming economy. If you don't have a good supporting cast, you will never grow and develop the company. Remember, people don't leave their jobs they leave their managers. If you have the best in class team, the rest will come together.

What is your earliest memory of success?

Creating our first sales team. When I started Window Nation, I ran all of the appointments until we became too busy. That is when I was forced to hire more people BUT I wanted everyone to be like me and close at a high level. I know I couldn't replicate myself, but I created a group of 6 talented sales reps which allowed us to take the company to the next level of growth. Something extremely hard to achieve in our business when you have no track record in the market and trying to get people to take the leap of faith to work here. I spent countless hours in training them to become the best they could be.

CHAPTER 8

Exercise to Be A Leader

"Nothing will work unless you do."

- John Wooden

There aren't many things in this life that have as much impact on success as exercise does. That said, I hate to place a greater emphasis on which "Make It Count" principle is more important than the next. But with the power of exercise, across so many disciplines, it could be said that nothing else is more important in life.

We are given one, and only one, vessel during this journey. The problem is that with developing economies and technology, we are moving less and less. We can now order groceries from home, and don't even have to get out of our pajamas, to be ready for a work conference call in bed. We can text our friends instead of having to meet for a coffee. We can sit longer, watching our favorite shows from 10 different media outlets — all while creating destructive time habits. There will be a day when Artificial Intelligence and Anti-Aging hackers make it possible, with simple solutions, to extend our lives by dozens of years. Although we have definitely developed concepts over the years to help extend life, they still doesn't exist just yet in 2018.

The main concepts still exist today as they have for a long time: a solid eating plan (not a diet, as that is a form of restriction that does not last), outlets for mental stress, relationships built on mutual respect, and the most important factor: exercise. Being a doctor for over a decade has taught me that the patients who typically do well in the long haul, are the ones that submit to a habit of exercise. The human body was designed for one thing, and that is *movement*. This chapter could be a whole book by itself, on the physiological benefits of exercise (although, I think for most that would be like watching paint dry.)

Instead, the goal of this chapter is to explain why exercise is so important to our daily journey. It is also about the overall positive effect that it has on our lives. We have all watched a movie where an expedition team finds some kind of secret map. It's a map that has been hidden for centuries, and its graph will lead the team on an adventurous, scary, twisting journey to find the infamous "fountain of youth." This journey doesn't exist just in the movies, but happens every day in real life, as well, the "fountain of youth" is nothing more than exercise. The problem is we come up with excuses for why it *doesn't work* in our lives.

As a doctor, I have heard about every excuse in the book. My response is always the same: "You have the time, you've just picked something else to do." That's right. We *all* have the time to dedicate 30-60 minutes to exercise, 3-5 days a week, but we love to drive the excuse train right past the importance of exercise in our lives. Think about your daily routine. I am constantly breaking my day down with a question: "Was I efficient that day or not?"

The key to "Making It Count" each day is in being sure that you are not missing out on the things that matter most, due to a lack of discipline. This theory goes right into the eye of the argument storm — the one that says, "I don't have time to exercise." Here are just a few observations that I have made over my years about habits that would allow you to make that extra space in your day, to fit in one of the most important things for your health:

- Wake up 30 minutes earlier.
- Check social media half as much as you do each day (I am sure that will free up at least 30 minutes.)
- Read your school book while walking on the treadmill.
- Skip stopping for that coffee and make it at home instead. This will give you the extra time that it took you to drive to coffee shop and wait in line.
- Stop texting your friend about your day's problems and, instead, ask them to go for a walk.
- Schedule a yoga, spin, or Pilates class somewhere that will cause you to lose money if you skip it. This will definitely make you think twice and will create an accountability clause with a loved one -- telling them that you will make time to invest in your health.

I have read hundreds of books on successful individuals over the years. I have studied their habits and their traits to find out what makes them tick, because I have always been interested in figuring out how to improve myself.

Do you know what all these successful people have in common?

You are correct if you said exercise.

Exercise is the common habit within all of their structures of success. Some of these people are the cream of the crop, in regards to being the world's most successful individuals. They carry travel, business, and personal schedules that make most of their daily routines very simple. Yet despite how busy they are, there is no argument as to whether or not they can find the time for exercise. It just isn't an option *not* to.

One thing that technology and business growth has created is the expanding option to exercise anywhere in the world at any time. The amount of fitness specific studios, gyms, equipment at hotels, online programs, and the depth of what mother nature offers is vast and extensive across all platforms in this life. Can't get to a gym? Then go for a walk. Can't go for a walk because the weather is bad? Then stay in your living room and do squats and pushups for a set time period. With all of this information, it becomes obvious that time is the weakest of excuses for us to not exercise.

I find that the easiest way to structure exercise into your routine is to find the strongest benefit for doing it — something so strong that if you don't exercise, you know that you're not just letting *yourself* down, but you're also affecting whatever it is you so strongly associate with needing to put the effort in.

I will go over more benefits shortly, but my personal number one is family. My time invested into making sure I exercise daily helps me with many micro improvements. But the macro in my life is to do all I can to be around for as long as possible. While I know things could end tomorrow — and that's what makes the "Make It Count approach so powerful — I also know that with the right tools in my tool box, I can help in extending my life should I be given the opportunity to live so long. My commitment to my time is because of how it relates to helping my kids and wife.

We need to find a reason to be connected to everything we do. Any habit worth doing, requires energy to help us propel down the path. While caffeine and some other remedies can provide temporary energy, there is nothing more natural than the power of exercise. You think Richard Branson, founder of over 400 companies, thrives off of a cup of joe? He has gone on record numerous times stating that he couldn't be the energetic game changer he is without staying consistent to his exercise routine.

When we live in the "Make It Count" mindset, we are pulling together ways to live each day with the maximum potential we can generate. Wouldn't it be easier to produce those results if we felt young and full of energy? This is why we refer to exercise as the "fountain of youth" in the "Make It Count" circle. The benefits cross just about every spectrum of what makes our life better each day. Exercise benefits include: weight control, improved mood, prevention against health conditions, better sleep, raised self-esteem, and increased energy. I've heard it said that a half hour of exercise has similar effects to taking an antidepressant. It boosts happiness levels, teaches goal setting behaviors, improves memory, helps us live longer and become leaders. The list within my notes goes on for another three pages, but let's stick with this short list for now. It covers the most foundational basis for future success.

More specifically, there are five "fountain of youth" staples that we focus most on within the "Make It Count" lifestyle:

1. **Benefit from habits, schedules, and goals.** — Improvement in the ability to make the most of your routine, comes straight from habits. I always tell my patients that the only way they will get better is to make what I am teaching them a habit. If they only invest a small portion of their life into improving, then it

may either take a very long time or it may never happen at all. Formatting an exercise habit into your schedule helps you to chase goals you never thought were possible. Habit number one could be waking up a half hour earlier, to go for a quick run. This habit, done consistently, can go on to improve your schedule to the point where you are not running out the door in a frazzled state every morning. This, in turn, puts you to work early and full of energy from your morning accomplishments. Thus, you are able to carry more personal growth towards everything you do which makes you and those around you better. Others will then notice when you land the dream job you were chasing.

2. **Exercise helps improve balance.** — How many times have you gotten to a place where your stress and anxiety seem to outweigh your will to be positive and upbeat? A formal exercise routine, inserted into your day with consistency, has the ability to balance out these negative emotions. The greatest moments of creativity in my life have come to me on a long run. The solo focus of being out on the roads, pursuing a better well-being, has always been a foundation to help me with decision making. The problem with stress and anxiety is that we typically don't have outlets to let them free. Some outlets only produce more anxiety. Exercise always provides an outlet for achievement, but it also provides a way to balance out negative emotions. It gives you the time to figure out what your next move will be toward personal success.

3. **Exercise builds discipline.** — Exercise is great at breaking down destructive habits. When you cross the threshold into making exercise a habit, you are also crossing the threshold into building a solid foundation for discipline. Hitting the snooze button 10 times becomes a thing of the past. Letting yourself off the hook for missing a workout for no reason becomes a thing of the past. Allowing yourself to eat a terrible diet becomes a thing of the past. And coming up with excuses for your lack of time becomes a thing of the past too. Exercise brings forth a promise to yourself to be better in all aspects of life: mind, body, and spirit. Each of these benefits from the perks of making yourself sweat a little. I know now, that if the thought of skipping a workout comes up, I won't let myself off the hook. I will press forward, as the reward outweighs the temporary weakness.

4. **Exercise breaks down limitations.** — There are not many choices in our life that have the potential to boost our confidence on a regular basis. There was a time when I thought that racing an Ironman was impossible. I couldn't run a 50 mile trail race, and there was no way I could compete in a CrossFit competition.

Most of these personal limitations were based of genetically bad feet. However, with each challenge I sat down and wrote out a plan of how I was going to get there and decided why not. It was the day-to-day grind of exercise and fitness that allowed me to build the confidence to think that I could not only get over these feats, but maybe even do them well. The excuse in my head was strong, but my will and ability to routinely test my fitness gave me the confidence to grow as an individual.

5. **Exercise shows us how to work smarter and not harder**. — The belief that time is a precious commodity has been repeated over and over on the "Make It Count" path. I could write "time is precious" for about 200 pages, over and over, and it's likely that we would still take time for granted. Patients of mine who are struggling with an exercise routine always complain about time. They don't have several hours each day to pursue what they know is important. Unless you're a single person, with little commitment, not many people have several hours (not that it would be the most efficient use of someone's time). The goal with any project is to work smarter, not harder. When I trained for my first Ironman, I thought bigger was better. I probably put in 20-25 hours per week of training. The result was that I finished, but I was nowhere near my goal. Fast forward to ten years later, and I have three kids. I have a busy practice, the third kid was just born, and I have many more responsibilities than before. With the right plan and the goal of working *smarter*, I averaged about 8-10 hours per week of training. I reached an Ironman personal record (PR) of well over a three-hour improvement. Exercise doesn't have to be a part-time job. You simply need to get into the routine of doing something that pushes your heart, you mind, and your body to start moving.

We live in an age where diabetes is on a rise in our youth. Part of this comes from what they are eating, but an even bigger part comes from the fact that kids don't move as much as they used to. Between video games, TV, a lack of daily physical activity in school, and barely going outside and playing after school, movement has been stripped from our youth. My wife and I have made a pact that exercise will always be a bonding point with our kids. We do CrossFit workouts together, go on hikes together, run 5K's together, go swimming together and we set goals as to how they feel after working out on a consistent basis.

Don't overlook the impact you have on your kids when they see you taking care of yourself. Leadership skills focus on clarity, vision, drive, and inclusion. When our youth see us sticking to a plan, trying to be better and "Making It Count," then it inspires them to lace up their shoes and follow in those footsteps.

Make It Count Foundations

1. WE ALL HAVE TIME! The time excuse for exercise needs to be put to rest. We all have time - you just picked something else to do in its place. Write down your schedule for a full week from waking up to going to bed and I guarantee you, with the right focus, you will find time.

2. There is no mistake that the most successful people in the world and the most successful people you know in your community take time to exercise.

3. Physical activity is the best way to improve cognitive function. Exercise helps you have a leg up on problem solving, decision making and focus.

4. Don't know where to start with your exercise journey? One of the things that makes fitness so great is that you can ask your neighbor, friend or family member what they are doing. Ask if you can tag along as a form of accountability. Doing something as a community makes anything more exciting and has a stickability factor of making you commit.

5. Doing anything well in life requires energy. Outside of temporary external factors like things you eat or drink. Exercise has the ability to provide you with a lifetime of free energy.

Make It Counter: Esther Collinetti

Esther has a fearless approach to life and thrives on taking risks. She started teaching group fitness classes in Baltimore in 2000 and has taught in all the city's major gyms and private studios. She completed her 200-hour yoga teacher training to further connect her client's minds, breath, and body while sweating on their bikes. This persistent passion for fitness enabled her to become a lululemon ambassador and, through lululemon's goal coaching program, Esther was able to establish clear visions and take action in order to live a life she loves. In 2013, she quit her full-time job as a research project manager to embark on her mission to open Baltimore's first cycle studio. In January 2014 REV Cycle Studio opened in the heart of Federal Hill and a second studio opened in Brewers Hill on February 2017. This badass uses cycling as a mode of motivation and personal growth to help you take the risks you never thought possible in pursuit of your fullest life. As a triathlete who has completed 9 Ironman races and also as a passionate entrepreneur, Esther is constantly pushing her own limits. Esther is now living her dream thanks to her fearless approach to life and is taking her mindful goal coaching to inspire many others in her community and around the world through fitness adventure retreats.

Esther was recognized as runner up for *"Best Group Fitness Instructor"* by Baltimore Magazine (2015, 2016 and 2017), *"Best Fitness Instructor"* by the Baltimore Sun (2017), and a *"40 Under 40"* honoree by the Baltimore Business Journal (2015).

Your passion for life and the challenges it presents are second to none. Where does that passion stem from?

My internal drive has been created since my childhood by many events. Where I grew up, the way my parents raised me, the brother and sister I had. All these factors created my drive to life. All these are emphasized by my fear of failure which is my motivator in life. I always test my limits by knowing my fear and heading in that direction. My fear points me to my true north.

You have crushed the entrepreneurial journey with a very successful indoor spinning operation called Rev Cycle. What have you learned during that journey that helped shape the person you are today?

REV Cycle Studio was my dream. I wanted nothing else in my life than to own and open my own spin studio in Baltimore. I wanted to create a space in which the community felt loved, appreciated, honored, welcomed, and adored each time they showed up. I wanted to also provide a safe space for clients and instructors, a space of love and respect. Soon after opening the doors of REV back in January 2014, I lived the next 6 months in complete misery. I lost myself in the dream. I was so invested and dedicated to the dream that I put everything else in my life at risk, including my health, my marriage, my friendships, my own family. I put everything on hold to make REV a success. This needed to happen with a new studio but I knew it was not going to be possible to sustain this lifestyle at the risk of losing all my other dreams like my marriage, health, etc. As REV grew and flourished, I was able to pull back and refined myself and my balance. I realized my biggest lesson in life is that in pushing so hard for one dream, you will put everything else at risk if you don't take care of your other dreams. I learned that it's okay to want what you want and to go for it, in all aspects of your life. That negotiating what you want is not possible if you are putting your own happiness at risk. I learned to be okay with sacrifices as long as you alert your support group, so you feel supported and so they don't feel you have abandoned them. I also learned the hard way that in pushing so hard for a dream you may lose all connection to what really matters the most in life which are the people you adore the most. At times I felt like REV was swallowing me, yet this was my dream, my baby. I had to relearn how to be me away from REV and to make sure there was both REV and there was also Esther. One is the business .. the dream.. and one is the human. This was a hard lesson to learn in the past 4.5 years.

What are your top three habits?

Stay inspired is my main one. If I am not inspired everything goes to shit. My WHY in life is to inspire others to take bold risks with their own lives. Therefore, I must stay inspired to be able to fulfill my story, my legacy. I am inspired by reading, taking yoga classes, meditating and taking workshops that can help me move past my own bullshit.

My next big habit is taking care of myself - meaning self-love. I make sure I treat myself to pleasures that I enjoy such as a long bubble bath with a book. A glass of expensive champagne. A lovely day at the spa. I give myself little gifts because I appreciate taking care of my body in ways that relax me. I do enough physical work, so, this is my time to be pampered for me and by me.

I keep a journal. Sometimes for a few months it's about gratitude, sometimes it's about my inner voice and how I sabotage my own self, it could also be more about clearing my slate each day… so it's more of a journal on things that I need now…. as life is a rollercoaster so the journal provides me space for me to write for letting go or filling me up.

If you could design a perfect day and live in that bubble, what would your perfect day look like?

Well so far, my perfect days so far in my life have been crossing the finish line of both of my full Ironmans, vacationing, being around loved ones… so these make my perfect days. Doing the things that I love the most: Racing. Family. Travel.

You are the queen of time management and could probably write a book on living a life of efficiency. If you only had two hours a day to focus on you, what would you do?

Goal coaching. Asking myself what do I want with my whole heart, and then make a plan to get shit done. It takes courage to answer this question and to put it in motion. That is when life rewards you, when you do what you love with your whole heart. This is time well spent investing in yourself to make sure you are on track to live the life you love.

What is the most difficult decision you have had to make in your life? How have you grown from it?

Quitting my lucrative job as a scientist to open a fitness studio. I had to think very deeply on the pros and cons especially regarding money. It was transformative and scary as shit! My lesson was that its okay to want what you want. Forget titles. Forget fear. Forget your education. Forget money. What the fuck do you want with all of your heart and go do that!

Make It Count

If you could put a saying on a billboard, what would it say?

Don't be a fucking pussy mother fucker.

What do the words "Make It Count" mean to you?

That no matter what happens never give up on your dream.

CHAPTER 9

Non-Negotiables

"It's not a goal!!! It's non-negotiable."

- Lori Schaefer

Non-negotiable: not open to discussion or modification.

When I was young, I wasn't sure that I had any non-negotiables in my life. I knew that eating, sleeping, playing sports, and watching sports were common avenues of energy expenditure each day. However, I wouldn't say that I truly held myself accountable to each one — at least, not in the same fashion that I hold my non-negotiables now.

The biggest success killer in today's world is the vivid world of distraction. Distraction is anything that takes us away from our goals. Distraction is the procrastination that is so present in our daily rituals. Any direction you turn, you can almost guarantee yourself some form of distraction. Some forms are incredibly strong, while others are weak. But even the weak ones build upon themselves until you have made a so-called mountain out of a molehill.

The key to escaping this world of distraction and accomplishing your success points is incorporating some sound, non-negotiable principles into your life. This is a list of things that you won't tolerate the absence of; things that you don't even think about, that you just do because they are immovable objects on your path to success. These are the things you hold yourself accountable to. They are the rock of your foundation that stop you from sliding into a world of mediocrity. Once that slide starts, it is often tough to reverse that trajectory. The footing is not great; there is nothing to grab onto, our hopes diminish, and we fall into a world of faulty expectations.

Non-negotiables allow us to have a strong footing in constant forward momentum. Remember, the goal is to constantly be growing by at least 1% each day. When the momentum is constantly going forward, then the distractions become fainter and smaller. Procrastination becomes a foreign word and you are constantly looking forward to any and all challenges presented to you. The goal is to define your non-negotiables and to cement them into your daily habits, rituals, and paradigms. When you do this, you stop thinking of your non-negotiables directly, but instead focus on excluding the thoughts and actions that go against them.

At 42 years old, my non-negotiables are different than they were when I was 25. And I know they will be different when I am 55, too. What stays the same is how important they are to my attack on everything in my life.

My TOP TEN Non-Negotiables in 2018:
1. I will put family first. (Always shower them with love!)
2. I will exercise daily.
3. I will eat clean about 80% of the week.
4. I will read for 60 minutes each day.

5. I will value optimism.
6. I won't tell anyone they *can't* achieve something.
7. I won't accept a meeting, without an agenda. (Time is precious.)
8. I won't gossip.
9. I will smile, even when I don't feel like it.
10. I will work hard at everything I do, so that no excuse will stop me.

When we lock in our non-negotiables, we develop a sound confidence as to what is in our best interest. These values also secure one of the most important commodities we have in life: TIME! Time is the only commodity that we can't make more of. We can't guarantee anything past what we are currently reading. Yet, the decisions we make on a daily basis are geared toward what will be best for us tomorrow — or maybe next week, or 5 years from now.

I am all in favor of having long term goals for your mission in life. However, I also think that the act of putting things off is a major mistake. Having solid non-negotiables allows us to base our decisions on what is best for those items, *right now*. I try to think what these would have been when I was 16, 17, or 18 years old. I even try to think what they might be for someone at the same age in 2018, as times have definitely changed.

I suspect that they could potentially look like this:

Non-Negotiables for a 16 Year Old in 2018:
1. I will stop comparing my life to others (i.e. social media, groups and sports).
2. I will find a mentor and mirror their actions.
3. I will work hard, knowing that regret hurts more than hard work in the moment.
4. I will volunteer my time to those less fortunate, as caring is a all-important action.
5. I will form solid friendships with people who push me to grow and not fade.

The impact of these 5 values, I know for a fact, would build upon everything that I could do and participate in throughout my journey. The problem that I had, when I was that age, was not a hindrance of hard work. Actually, it was a hindrance in that I thought the world revolved around me. Each action I made had a sole purpose in that it was going to help me. My only non-negotiable was *me*, me, me, and not *others*.

At some point along the way, we have to learn that in order to be successful and grow, we'll need to have a team on our side. That team is made up of each person we come into contact with throughout our day. Our team could, of course, be a wife or husband, our family, our neighbor, our colleagues, or even our teammates. When our non-negotiable is to "Make It Count" each and every day, then everyone we come into contact with can be a meaningful person on our team. Actively ask the person at the grocery store how they are doing, and it shows them that people care. It opens their life to possibility. You never know when their possibility might become part of your journey.

The "Make It Count" mentality does not favor burning bridges, as a burnt bridge is a closed door to possibility. Non-negotiables aren't on our conscious minds, as they are meant to be habits ingrained into our doing. We wake up early because it's productive. We open a door or regularly say thank you because manners are a priority. We make time for exercise because being healthy for the team is a top priority.

Non-negotiables are *necessary* for the growth that you are searching for. In order to "Make It Count," to live a life geared toward maximizing your time and helping others, there are certain things that need to be put on an autopilot of sorts. These can't be things we need a "to-do list" to help us remember. They can't be things we forget to do, as they are the foundational structure of everything we do. Take exercise, for example. It is the foundation for health, wellness, happiness, gratitude, leadership, and many more valuable qualities. If daily exercise is not one of your non-negotiables, you will always find a reason to bypass its importance. It has to be so strong in significance, that you never budge. It has to be so crucial that you write your script around doing exercise. It has to be so strong that you won't sacrifice it to do something else in its place.

Non-negotiables can be whatever you desire them to be. The key is not to let them in and out of your life, whenever you please. But rather, have them as a part of every move, every decision, and every action you take. One of my kids' non-negotiables is that they call every adult either Mr. or Ms. — as a show of respect, confidence, and trust. They don't think of it anymore; it comes naturally for them, and it's an important piece of who they are.

Make It Count Foundations

1. Non-negotiables are the foundation of what makes us who we are. They are actions that we produce on a daily basis, which allow us to grow effectively and efficiently over time.
2. Distraction is the king of side-tracking your dreams. When we have strong non-negotiables we give ourselves a layer of armor to fight against distraction.
3. What are your top 10 non-negotiables? I challenge you to come up with a list of 10 things that are incredibly important to you — things that you will not waiver from, no matter the distraction trying to sway you.
4. We are never too old to have non-negotiables. The earlier the non-negotiables are placed within our daily structure, the quicker they become a piece of our successful future. Take the lesson from this chapter and use it to help those around you develop their strong non-negotiables — to help them "Make It Count" a little easier each day.
5. Non-negotiables should not be a stressful implementation into your routine. These should be actions that you deem important, necessary, and integral in helping define who you are and what you want to do in life.

Make It Counter: Cheryl Endicott Schwitzgebel

I'm a medical anomaly. When doctors meet me for the first time and begin reading my medical records, I love watching their eyes get bigger in disbelief that I'm still alive...and thriving after all these years!

My story begins as I was born with a ventricular septal defect (VSD) in my heart or heart murmur. It's quite common and 1 in 1,000 people have them. It was monitored but never surgically repaired. I was told that (later in life) something might happen.

As luck would have it, at 11 years of age I developed a brain aneurysm. Doctor's were quick to act after I suffered from severe headaches and a seizure. The only residual effect is I wear glasses, but I'm not sure if that was caused by it or not.

Only 9 months later (6 days after my 12th birthday), I suffered a spinal stroke at T3 level (mid back). Although I've been told it's unrelated, I have my suspicions. At the time, I lost use of both legs & my left arm. Fortunately, I was able to recover the use of my arm and only have to use a manual wheelchair.

Like most people, I went through the various stages of grief after becoming paralyzed. Unlike most, I've come to realize the many things that have happened are actually blessings in disguise. I've been able to do so many things BECAUSE it happened that I would never have done otherwise. Because of that I believe I have become a better person.

When I initially ended up in the wheelchair, my dad told me there was nothing really wrong with me. I just had to use 4 wheels to get around instead of 2 legs. I could still be anything I wanted to be. It was that belief that has led me to dream big and achieve lofty goals.

When I was in physical therapy, my mom used to sing the Diet Pepsi jingle, "You can do it! We can help. One calorie. One calorie. Diet Pepsi can help!" I can still hear her singing it! At the time, I hated that song, but it would get me fired up and I'd push myself harder. It was the support and love of my family and friends that helped push me into achieving later on. It's that attitude that I've developed and used to motivate me for the rest of my life. If there's anyone who tells me I can't do something, I'll do it just to prove them wrong. The only one who can tell me I can't is ME. And (according to my dad) CAN'T means WON'T.

Each year, on September 29th, I actually celebrate the day I became a wheelchair user. I call it my Chapter 2. My life took a drastic turn that day that I know greatly impacted my life and the person I would become. It was a "make you or break you" moment. You can either let it break you and wallow in self-pity, or let it make you and do great things with your life. I always prefer making something better, because no one wants to be around someone feeling sorry for themselves. We all have something to deal with in our lives.

Today, now that I'm older, I'm no longer able to wheelchair race but I continue working out and "moving on."

Noteworthy things I've done:
- Had a successful career in Corporate Journalism and Technology
- Traveled across the country from East to West coast
- Competed in numerous 5k, 10k, Half Marathons and the Chicago Marathon
- Tried out for the 1996 Paralympics
- Carried the Olympic Torch at the site of the 1996 Olympics

What is the biggest lesson you have learned in life?

Treasure each day...each person...each lesson...each love...each loss. Treasure it because you're alive to experience it. Some lessons are easy, but the hardest ones teach us the most. And if you don't learn something, then you've wasted an opportunity to grow and become better.

You had a life-altering experience that put you in a wheelchair. Most people would potentially quit and live a life of "poor me." Do you believe that life happens for you and not to you? How have you managed to be such a positive influential person?

When bad things happen, people often blame God. They ask "Why do you let bad things happen?" In the movie "Oh God," John Denver asks God (George Burns) why he lets bad things happen. God says he can't prevent bad things from happening. They have to happen. What he can do is make something good come from it. That's how I look at it. In my case, I look at all the many blessings that I've experienced where that is exactly the case! I've met people & done things that I never would have if I would not have ended up in the wheelchair. I tried out for the Paralympics and met Jackie Joyner-Kersee, while I was being honored. I've been on local television for carrying the Olympic Torch and hosted the sports cast! I think because I'm grateful & feel truly blessed, I attract people who are seeking it.

What do you do when you feel overwhelmed?

At those times, I disconnect from technology, people and take some time for myself. I love going for a "walk" in my chair or ride on my handcycle. Nature often centers me. It's where I feel connected with God. I also like to surround myself with other positive people and do something fun, like play games or hang out with close friends.

What is your definition of success?

It's knowing I made a positive difference in someone's life. It could be something as simple as sharing a smile with someone who looks like they needed it. Small gestures can make the biggest impacts even if we don't see the outcome.

What advice would you give a younger version of yourself?

Live fully and completely. There are so many things I didn't do and wished I'd had, because I was scared or didn't have the money. As Nike says, "Just do it!" Find a way to make it happen now...not later.

What advice would you give someone who had an accident and now has to adjust to a new norm?

Don't let anyone tell you that you can't. Doctors. Nurses. Family. Friends. In fact, do it despite the fact that they tell you that. My dad (a Marine) always said "Can't means won't." When people tell me that, I use it as means for motivation. I have never considered myself "disabled" or "handicapped." It's just an inconvenience.

Do you feel like people put limitations on you because of the wheelchair? What habits do you consistently perform to outweigh those societal views?

Yes, I do, and it hurts, because I know what I'm capable of accomplishing. Before I even have a chance to prove myself, I've been told I'm basically worthless. The only cure is education. Until you personally know someone with a physical impairment, you have no idea what they are capable of doing (or not doing). I feel that's my purpose in life...to educate.

What does a perfect day look like for you?

Every day is a perfect day! When I was younger, I used to think it was graduating or my wedding day. Now that I'm older, it's every day, because each day is a gift. So often we take each day for granted, but you never know when you'll no longer have tomorrow.

What do the words "Make It Count" mean to you?

If you're going to do something, put yourself all in. Give 110%. Go all the way and make it mean something, otherwise why do it? Make it mean something to you and don't just go through the motions.

CHAPTER 10

Steal the Mirror

"Make a list of the people you admire and what makes them amazing. Then go out and become those things yourself."

-Tai Lopez

I recently read a quote by Pablo Picasso which goes, "Good artists copy, great artists steal." There is so much truth to this quote and I feel it speaks to the idea of "stealing the mirror." We live in an age where information is at our fingertips in every fashion and medium imaginable.

When I was a kid, having a mentor meant that you had to physically meet with someone who would give you the tips, tools, and tactics to help you approach your life in a more efficient way. Personally, I still believe that this is the most beneficial way to engage in personal development. Having a physical, face-to-face mentor allows each person to engage in true emotional development. Nothing is more important than the energy that is transmitted between these two individuals.

However, in today's fast-moving technological age, we have the advanced option of having numerous mentors from many different facets of life at our fingertips. As previously mentioned in this book, there is a popular idea that we are the average of the five people with whom we spend the most time with. But personally, I believe that we are the average of the five people with whom we associate the most. While human interaction is number one, we now have the ability to associate with great writers through various outlets; watch great speakers break down barriers on YouTube and in TedTalks; listen to podcasts where other people interview the greats; engage with incredible seminars on dozens of new platforms. From multiple new outlets, we have the capacity to learn which habits the world's most successful people operate through.

This is where the "steal the mirror" concept is derived from. Identify what it is that your idols are doing and weave those actions into your inner fabric. This way, when you look into the mirror, you will see those successful characteristics dressed in your own clothes. When you can "steal the mirror" away from successful people in history, you get a crash course on the simple habits, routines, and mindset that have generally worked in the past. Once you can see these abilities in yourself, then you can start focusing on the extra foundational metrics that will make you *special*. These metrics will set the stage for others — those now looking to "steal *your* mirror."

As you can see, the trend here is to work together — other-people focused — in order to be successful. Living a "Make It Count" lifestyle is not about belittling others or telling others that what they do is a waste of time. The goal is to unite as one, to learn from each other about the impactful ways we can work together, to teach each other the simplest routines for success.

When I went to chiropractic school, the course work was challenging. But, as we all know, textbooks can only teach us so much. So what did I do? I looked for the most successful doctor in my circle and I searched for exactly what it was that made him tick.

This gave me the foundation for how to treat patients in the physical sense, which allowed me to be a step ahead of some of my classmates at graduation. Once that first real-world patient had entered my office, I knew I already had the successful foundational elements from someone else's mirror. Then it was up to me to perfect the art of how Dr. *Jake* treated patients.

There is no shame in asking for help, or for mentorship, or for someone to guide you along your path. However, there *is* shame in *not* growing — especially in an age when it's so easy to connect with anyone in just seconds. You would be amazed at how quickly people want to help, if you just ask. At age 41, my one big regret is that I didn't find more mentors back in my teen years. Not having the cognitive recognition to know that someone I look up to — someone who I want to be like, someone I follow — could very easily take me under their wing, if I only asked.

There is no need to go on this journey all by yourself. "Stealing the mirror" allows us to broaden our horizons further than ever before. Last week, I read a book on Thomas Edison. I listened to a podcast from Tim Ferriss. I listened to a book on growth mindset. I had coffee with three extremely successful entrepreneurs. I treated 100 patients. I worked out with five highly competitive professional athletes, and I kicked a soccer ball around with my daughter. I gave a speech on effective habits and spoke with six people on the phone about the "Make It Count Lifestyle Project." I also watched my wife interact with sales clients. And all of that was just half of the week. If I hadn't come away stealing something from each and every situation, then I wouldn't have been maximizing my time. Each and every situation we cross gives us an opportunity for growth.

I never liked speaking in front of people, but now I love it because it's like sport. Each time I speak, I grow. I take a step into an uncomfortable arena of life, and I learn how I can be better. Nothing can replace the personal process of starting a company, having the passion to grow something you 100% identify with, and learning the ups and down of the journey as you go. You grow enormously just because you have to. I recommend that along the journey from idea generation to fruition, you take a few 5-minute breaks to see how your mentors can help you. This accountability will keep you laser focused on reaching the success you desire. Having that palpable force of support around you is what the "steal the mirror" concept focuses on. Don't go the whole journey by yourself but bring along those who have blazed down a similar path and succeeded. They will have priceless information to offer you, which could potentially help you avoid getting lost in the wrong rabbit hole.

Dreams are the most magical thing we can invest our time in during our journey to build our legacy. Dreams allow us to fight for something bigger than who we are at this moment in time. My oldest daughter dreams of being a professional soccer player someday. She says it with confidence, and she puts all her energy eggs into the same single basket of effort when she steps onto the practice field. She and I have had the conversation a few times; that while hard work is an important friend in this dream, it is still very helpful to reach out to those who have achieved it in the past. She has had the life privilege of knowing a few professional soccer players and she "steals their mirrors" every day. She mimics the professional attitude needed to succeed: the humble mentality that there is always more work to be done, the desire to always stay thirsty for more, the thick skin to learn from failure without taking it personally, and the knowledge that keeping all of these growth factors in place will consistently help her become a better person.

"Stealing The Mirror" can be broken down into three key stages:

1. **Identify your mentor** — Knowing what you want to do, what your dreams are, and what you're passionate about is the first step. Next, find someone in that domain or expertise that you admire or look up to. If the person is alive and you have the ability, reach out to them with gratitude and let them know how much their journey means to you. Don't just ask them to help you, but find a way to offer them something in return. People love a relationship that is mutually beneficial, and not just a one-way street. If they are not alive, then grab a book and learn everything you can about this individual.

2. **Study, learn, and grasp** — Once you have identified your mentor, or mentors, take the time to study their tools, their tactics, and the practices they use for daily success. What habits do they focus on most that lead to a better version of themselves? Your interviewing skills will have to be opened up and practiced if you have the chance to go face-to-face with a mentor. If not, no worries. We live in such a technological age where information on greats like Rockefeller, Edison, and Franklin are just a click or a read away.

3. **Visualize their success in your shoes** — Now that you are armed with this knowledge and you can identify which principles resonate best with your mission, you can look in the mirror and see some of their successful habits in your own life. You can look in the mirror with confidence, knowing that you have been equipped with the right tools for change, the tactics for success, and the metrics for a better life.

"Stealing the mirror" is just one option within the "Make It Count" lifestyle approach. Life is about efficiency and consistency; the more efficient we are with our time, the more productive we can be on a daily basis. The more consistent we are in life, the more we can learn what does and does not work. Many of our habits are specific to one individual, but there are other habits that have been tried over hundreds of years that never seem to fade from the foundation of greatness. When we can see these habits in others and then integrate them into our own fabrics, we soon become more efficient and consistent in our journey to "Making It Count."

Make It Count Foundations

1. Have you ever had a mentor? If not, identify someone in your community who is doing what you would like to do in life. Approach this person with a genuine desire to learn.

2. When you look in the mirror, what do you see? Can you visualize success factors from great inventors, entrepreneurs, and coaches in history? Take one principle from someone you admire, and then have a look at yourself in the mirror. Do you see improvement?

3. Maximizing your time within the "steal the mirror" principle is key to taking away as much knowledge as you can. Next time you're on a drive, listen to a podcast. Go for a run while playing your favorite audiobook. You could even dedicate your 15 minute lunch break to reading.

4. Not everything will fit into who you are. If you read about a habit that someone has but you can't see yourself making that habit, then maybe it's not right for your approach. In the end, the habit needs to mesh with your mission in life. If it doesn't, then you will never grab the concept because it's not authentic to you.

5. Visualization is an incredible tool for many facets of life. We can visualize so many pathways, along with what might happen down those pathways. Visualize how a habit, a tool, or a tactic will improve your life. This visualization will open up your spectrum to what is possible, thus allowing you to know when, where, and how to use the habit.

Make It Counter: Chris Miltenberg

In six seasons, Franklin P. Johnson, Director of Track and Field, and men's cross-country coach Chris Miltenberg has built Stanford into national championship contenders in both cross country and track and field.

In 2018, the Stanford women were a close third in the NCAA Outdoor Championships -- two points from first -- in the closest first-through-third team finish in meet history. It matched Stanford's highest women's finish ever, and the Cardinal men were eighth. The average place of 5.5 was Stanford's highest combined finish ever.

Taking into account NCAA team finishes in cross country, and indoor and outdoor track and field, the Stanford women received the Terry Crawford Program of the Year award. Stanford was the only school in the top three of both the men's and women's Program of the Year standings.

Under Miltenberg, the Pac-12 Coach of the Year, Stanford's cross country teams have combined for 12 NCAA team appearances, six NCAA podium finishes, four region titles, and a Pac-12 championship. Individually, Stanford has crowned 17 All-Americans who have combined for 25 All-America honors, seven NCAA top-10 individual finishes and four Pac-12 individual titles.

He twice has been named NCAA West Region Coach of the Year in cross country, in 2013 and 2016. He has coached 56 Stanford All-Americans to a total of 171 All-America honors. Of those, 37 have become first-team track and field All-Americans, earning a total of 62 first-team All-America honors

In 2016, both his men's and women's cross country recruiting classes were ranked No. 1 in the nation by Flotrack.

In track and field, Miltenberg's Stanford teams have combined for 12 top-20 NCAA team finishes indoors and outdoors. In 2015, his men's track and field recruiting class was named No. 1 in the nation by MileSplit.

Academically, Stanford's programs have excelled under Miltenberg, with recent runner earning a Rhodes Scholarship.

Stanford has earned the USTFCCCA Men's Scholar-Athlete of the Year in cross country in each of the past three years.

Miltenberg arrived from Georgetown, where he coached the Hoya women to the 2011 NCAA cross-country title.

At Georgetown, Miltenberg was the associate head coach for track and field and the head women's cross-country coach. He was named the USTFCCCA National Women's Cross Country Coach of the Year for 2011.

In five seasons at Georgetown, Miltenberg coached 36 All-Americans in track and field, an NCAA champion at 3,000 and 2016 Olympian. Miltenberg also led the Georgetown women to the 2012 Big East indoor track title.

Miltenberg is a 2003 graduate of Georgetown where he was a two-time All-American and placed fourth at the 2001 NCAA Indoor Championships in the 3,000. He went on to run professionally for a year with Adidas while training for the 2004 U.S. Olympic trials.

A native of Huntington, N.Y., he attended John Glenn High where he was a two-time scholastic All-American in the mile and was the New York state cross country runner-up. He won the mile at the 1998 Golden West Invitational.

You have built up two incredible programs at Georgetown and Stanford. What has been the foundation of your coaching that has allowed you to achieve consistent success?

If there has been a foundation to our success it has been always focusing on the process of growing and developing every single day, both for our athletes but also me as a coach; seeing every challenge, defeat or even failure (we've had plenty!) as an opportunity to learn, grow and get better. It took me a long time to mature to really having that mindset and it didn't fully crystallize to me until a few years ago (and a massive low point) how important it was for me to model that in my own behavior for my athletes to be able to really do it themselves. I put so much pressure on myself, especially when I first came to Stanford, that I lost sight of this growth mindset too often and my teams would reflect that in their own behaviors. We have core tenets we believe in, most of all that it is always about relationships and connecting with and really understanding each of my athletes where they are right now; not where I want them to be but where they are so I can help them move one step closer to being the best version of themselves. We have these core tenets but, arguably, just as important, we are constantly growing and evolving and embrace the process of doing that even when it's hard, it's scary or it hurts.

You have coached some of the best collegiate runners in recent years. Have you noticed a common theme amongst these athletes that sets them apart, besides athletic talent?

The common theme which I'd say exists in all my most successful athletes is an innate belief in themselves that they will reach their goals eventually even if they are not getting immediate results. The ones that stagnate are the ones that need the immediate results to have validation in both themselves and the process and when they don't get it, they start dulling the edge of their commitment ever so slightly. The great ones I've had innately believed in themselves enough to have the grit and resilience to weather the crucial hard period of growing and setbacks that they have to go through early in their career. The great ones can have their heart broken and not be afraid to love again, to go all in again in pursuing their goals with no guarantees it's going to work out. So few people can really do that! Our sport is a cumulative sum game and rewards long term focus and persistence; you have to believe in yourself and the system when the results aren't coming yet. This ultimately also made them the most coachable athletes because they trusted and believed in the process, me and themselves.

What is your definition of success?

From a coaching perspective, I define success as empowering and reaching each of my athletes to help them become the very best version of themselves they can possibly be, and, most importantly, leaving our program better prepared for any challenges that come in life ahead. Overall, success to me is constantly growing, learning and evolving through both struggles and victories and using that experience to impact others as much as possible. That to me is also learning from my life and past experiences and being better than maybe what I've gone through; that applies to how I approach being a Dad, which is ultimately my most important job of all!

What is your greatest failure? What did you learn from it?

I struggle with defining anything as my greatest "failure" just because I try as much as possible to see it as a growth opportunity and not even emphasize it as a failure. The place I would say I failed the most was that in my 5th year Stanford (2016-17). I put so much pressure on myself to have great results because it was "now an entire team of people I recruited, we should have it rolling by now etc. etc.". Basically, I was giving into external judgments of me and expectations and became focused on results to validate me as a coach instead of the process and, most of all, the people that I was responsible for leading. I gradually lost my way for about 6-8 months and our results, as well as the vibe in our locker room, reflected it. After finishing 2nd at the NCAA XC Championships in

November, we'd finish dead last at the Pac-12 Outdoor Championships that spring and only qualify one guy for the NCAA Outdoor Championships our worst results in my 7 years at Stanford and also, by far, the year we had the most injuries. I blame those injuries on myself and losing sight of being in touch with my guys and instead being more focused on the results, on "my results". That was all completely on me and it only got worse as the results got worse; it was a downward spiral I had to break myself and my guys wouldn't respond until I changed. Every time another injury popped up, I saw it more as these bad things were happening "to me" instead of seeing the bigger picture of my role in it. It really hit me after that season ended that I was so unhappy because of the way I was approaching coaching and the negative impact on my team was tangible. I either had to shift my mindset or get out of coaching! The biggest thing I re-learned (because I already knew it!) was to always stay focused solely on the people you're leading and doing the absolute best you can with them every day; to never let pursuit of my results make me gravitate from my principles and to always see challenges and setbacks as a great opportunity to learn and become a better, more complete coach, an opportunity to be grateful for. Most of all, to remember that it's not about me! And to be able to do that even if the public eye is watching, or you're being judged by people inside or outside of your organization. That's when it's more important than ever to stay true to yourself. It's also way more fun that way and the people you lead will respond to that!

What tools/tactics do you use to keep your athletes focused on the task or goal each season?

I approach it a bit differently. Our athletes are so goal oriented and live in such a results driven culture that we flip it the other way around and always remind them to stay focused on the process and the things they can control, like making our #1 goal to leave the NCAA Championships proud of who we are and how we have competed. That's a really high standard for us, the highest standard, higher than any result or even winning an NCAA title and it's one we're really honest with ourselves about when we reflect back, brutally honest when necessary. It's about the way we live every day in preparing, the way we maximize competitive opportunities, the way we have each other's backs and stick together in tough competitive situations. That is bigger than winning a national championship for us and that is all within our control so we come back to that at all times.

What is your favorite quote and why?

Treat success and failure as equal impostors - Rudyard Kipling - "If"
(this may not be exactly verbatim but it's how I've adapted it in my head over time!)

It serves as a reminder that things are never as good or as bad as you think they are and to be grateful for all the experiences, both successes and failures (or challenges) as part of your total story and as an opportunity to learn and get better. You've never got it all figured out and things are also never completely bad. It's your story, your masterpiece and it's all part of the learning and growth.

What piece of advice would you give a younger version of yourself?

To be patient and always enjoy where you are in the moment. Early in my career and even now at times, I'd catch myself getting caught up in where I'd end up next or what the next step was or how to go bigger and better. In many ways, having hard driving ambition is crucial but the best way to succeed is to be totally focused on what is right in front of you right now, to enjoy what's right in front of you, to be totally present because wherever you are, that's exactly where you're supposed to be at that moment, even when its hard or it's scary because you have no idea if the next step will come. My wife and I always look back and say how at every turn in our career and our family's growth, which were closely intertwined with all the moving etc., just when we were scared the next thing would never come or happen and we really needed it for our family, it always worked out and happened. That was in many ways luck but also a result of working really hard right where we were. I would go back and tell myself to enjoy it more and not let the ambition take away from enjoying the present and even the challenges as much as possible. That would definitely be what I'd also go back and tell myself as an athlete.
Have big goals but love the climb each day.

What do the words "Make It Count" mean to you?

It means living and doing everything you do with purpose and constantly learning, growing and evolving, constantly seeking out more challenge. Most of all, doing everything you can to impact other people and make them better. That is ultimately how you become the best version of yourself.

CHAPTER 11

Take Massive Action

"The path to success is to take massive, determined action."

- Tony Robbins

The title of this chapter seems pretty self-explanatory: take great action to accomplish whatever you most desire. The problem with big actions is that most people tend to take them only once. This chapter is geared toward **taking massive action** all the time.

Success is not just a one-time experience but something we can obtain with consistent, daily, massive action — or, like Tony Robbins says, "Massive, determined action." If we looked at a graph of people's actions towards their goals throughout the year, it would peak high in January and February and then start to taper down as the year went on. October, November and December would flatten out since, usually, by this point, people are pushing everything off to this mythical "New Year's resolution" idea. We have built it up in our head that if we start a new year with new goals, it will lead to a new version of us. It is more likely that those new year's resolutions will fail to help us progress toward the desired outcome we have in mind.

Why is this?

It is because we take massive action in January — to hit the gym, to eat better, and to sleep more. Then, as time progresses, the allure of that action starts to fade. We see progress, but not at the speed we desire. Or maybe we are just not as tied into the goal as we first thought. We stumble a little and we miss a few workouts. We stay up late and our cheat meals become our standard meals. The weight comes back on, we fall out of shape, and we start to feel a little tired. This chain reaction keeps up until the fall, when we simply give up in hopes that the next year's resolutions will be stronger. The problem is often that we haven't fully committed to the why. Part of taking massive action toward your goal is making the goals your everything. Tie the goal so deep into your roots that taking action toward achievement is your only option.

A couple of years ago, my now 12-year-old decided to go cold turkey and stop eating any pork products. Her decision was not based on any health ramifications, but simply on the fact that she loves pigs. She was 8 at the time, so we supported her even though we fully thought it was a phase. Surely bacon would stop her in her tracks eventually, right? But what happened was actually quite the opposite. She learned how to read labels, as pork products can be hidden in many different foods. She didn't push her goals onto anyone else; she wasn't trying to make other people feel bad for what they ate. She just stood strong in her own beliefs — sometimes even asking restaurants to verify exactly what was in a certain dish. She stayed true and, over a four year span, she has not cracked once. She has taken massive action: she had a strong reason to believe in achieving her goal and she brought people into her belief without causing any hard feelings. Even our family eventually stayed away from most things that contained pork.

While my daughter's pork avoidance might not be considered a huge or unrealistic goal to many, it was a big goal for her at 8 years old. Experience has taught me that in order to take massive action, we need to associate ourselves with challenging and unrealistic goals because they push us to attain a higher standard. Goals that are based in ease or comfort typically fade from one day to the next. They allow us to take a day off, ignore progress for a week or two, and they fail to ignite a fire in our belly that gets us up early in the morning to fight. Unrealistic goals are built to push us harder than we have ever been pushed before.

I understand the definition of unrealistic as something being uncommon amongst the common. It is the notion that something is not just difficult, but that it *cannot* be done -- people doubt your every move, or they don't believe in your chances. This is why I love applying it to everything. It's the same when someone says "impossible". The first thing I say is that the word itself has the word "possible" in it. Setting unrealistic expectations, goals, or dreams for ourselves forces us to dig deeper and reach higher than we ever have before. The more unrealistic the goal, the more knowledge, awareness, influence, and understanding we are forced to develop.

Every single guest writer in this book came to a breaking point in their lives. They decided one day to take massive action toward what they thought was most important for them, and they never looked back. They are difference makers. Not just because they had a great idea or a passion, but because they took massive actions that changed their lives for the better. The whole point of living for the moment is to help you clarify what your goals and objectives are. This allows you to have a specific purpose for your actions. With a specific purpose, you have your why. With a specific purpose, other people's opinions become your fuel for that extra push. With a specific purpose, you gain a mental clarity that helps you avoid the destruction of self-sabotaging thoughts.

"Vision without action is a daydream. Action without vision is a nightmare."
— Japanese Proverb

Taking massive action may sound great, but people typically end up doing something that I call "limitation of action." Comfort has become our kryptonite in the world of success. We hide behind comfort because doing something that makes us sweat — something that makes our stomach churn, or makes our hands shake — sounds awful. So we tend to hide behind the limitation of our actions. We subconsciously limit the actions needed, not because we decide we can't handle them, but because it lets us stay in our comfort zone.

Make It Count

Last week, I had a patient whose boss came to him and told him how well he has been doing at his job. He told him that at the upcoming national sales meeting, he would love for him to present his progress to roughly 800 people. And instead of saying yes — knowing the great, promotional opportunity this chance could give him — my patient didn't hesitate to tell his boss NO. His fear of getting up and being judged on a stage outweighed all of the positive outcomes that could happen in his life. He was afraid of getting out of his comfort zone. This was when I took off the doctor hat and put on the "Make It Count" hat. I told him that no matter what we do in life, we will always be judged by others. When we dream big, we will always get the attention of other people. So, the only option is to dream even bigger. I told him that the opportunity his boss presented to him was exactly what he had worked so hard for. The material was 100% in his wheelhouse, and the crowd would be there to learn from his vast boat of knowledge. I explained how he could practice within a smaller group setting, where the feedback would be more intimate. But, at the end of the day, I told him if he just took massive action toward crushing his speech, it would open up both his professional and personal worlds to advancing through uncomfortable moments. He could live the nightmare of having a fear of public speaking, without really knowing how the event would go. Or he could take immediate action to set himself up for an amazing event.

When we live a "Make It Count" lifestyle, we set ourselves up to expect more from ourselves. The expectation is that we will take massive action in any way and at any place we can, because it's what needs to be done. If its mid-October, we won't wait until January to do what could be done today. January might not come. And even if it does, we might be in a completely different place that makes our goal all the more challenging than it is today. The limitation of action creates a world where we just wait for things to happen. We wait for the job promotion, we wait for the motivation to workout, we wait for the book to write itself, we wait for the right moment to tell that one person we love them, and we wait on our dreams in hopes that they will come true with as little action as possible. I am sure there are cases of limitation that have provided people with success, but those stories are few and far between. Taking massive action on a consistent basis will extinguish the waiting game. Who wants to wait when we have no idea if the moment will ever be right? Who wants to wait when today could be our last day on this earth? Playing the waiting game is like betting in Vegas: the house always wins. And in this case, we lose all our hopes and dreams because life isn't going to make them happen for us.

Steps To Taking Massive Action

1. **Clarity in vision** — Taking massive action, repeatedly and consistently, becomes very difficult. We can all do something really big once, but doing it over and over again is the real grind. The key is to understand two things. The first is that this will not be a one time action. And the second is that we need to expect more out of ourselves. Having this expectation set in place — that we will go deep into the action plan and carry out our mission — will set the tone for everything that takes place next. Having the mental clarity to know you will be a "game changer" in your life, and in the lives of others, will help to grow your confidence in pursuing greatness in everything you do.

2. **Knowing your why** — Simon Sinek said it best, "It is one of life's greatest joys to wake up in the morning....every morning, with a clear sense of *why* that day matters, why every day matters." There really is nothing more powerful than finding your why. It becomes fuel for everything you do in life. All massive action is taken because you have found something in your journey that you are passionate about and it becomes the fabric of your mission. When I found the "Make It Count" lifestyle, it wasn't initially for anyone else but myself. I was in search of meaning beyond just smiling and living a great life. I wanted a purpose behind seeking the best in everything. I guarantee that when you find your why, you will jump out of bed in the morning with the energy of a king or queen. You will pursue your dreams without hesitation, and you will take people's opinions in stride — knowing that you are the only person to either accept them or move on. Taking massive action will be the only move you make.

3. **Comfort in failure** — I think we are arriving at a point in history where we are starting to realize that "failure" is not a bad word. Failure only means that we attempted something that didn't work, so it's back to the drawing board to figure out a better approach. Could you imagine a world if nothing ever failed? Life wouldn't be challenging, and thus nothing would push us to grow like we should. Failure is sometimes the only option on the road to taking massive action. When we push, push, push outside our comfort zone, we will fail at some point. That's when you do exactly as the chapter on failure tells you to do: smile and be confident in knowing that you just learned a strong life lesson for what to do better next time. Being comfortable with being uncomfortable, starts with accepting failure. You will swing and miss when taking massive action, but that

is completely fine. It just means that you are doing everything you can to "Make It Count."

4. **Action, Action, Action, Action** - The last step in taking massive action is jumping in and learning how to swim. When I was a kid, we lived on a river and across the street we had a spring-fed quarry. Water was everywhere, so my mom knew the importance of knowing how to swim. Option one was to drive to the pool, take lessons, and learn that way. Option two was to be thrown into the quarry water and take immediate massive action to learn how to swim in the moment. My mom took option two, and she threw my sisters and I into the quarry. Within days, we could swim on our own. There was no waiting patiently to learn at the pool. The fear of drowning was the why behind our massive action in that moment. Life is no different. In all the endeavors we pursue, there will be fear around corners, and that fear will try to tell us to take the safe route. Action is all we have that can take us to a new level of success. Without action, our goals and dreams are just nicely written words on a piece of paper.

Make It Count Foundations

1. Taking massive action requires consistency; it is not a one-time event. You need to be willing to do more than the average person does, and you need to expect more from yourself.

2. Start by setting challenging and unrealistic goals that push you to attain a higher purpose. Small goals require small actions, but enormous goals only require massive action.

3. Setting massive goals will help you develop an increased sense of knowledge, awareness, influence, and understanding of who you are and what your impact on the world will be.

4. It's natural to sit back on your dreams and rest. Hoping to find a better day when the opportunity might look prettier. This leads to regret and limitation of actions. We hold back on our actions because it doesn't feel right. Taking massive action squashes the limitation of actions mentality that is holding us back from the ability to make it count.

5. Finding your why will help any and all action taking in your future. You can watch Simon Sinek's Ted Talk video on finding your why as it's extremely powerful. Finding your why gives fuel to your action-taking and gives you a mission behind what you do.

Make It Counter: Doug Miller

I grew up in Huntingdon Valley, PA, a small town near Philadelphia. Throughout my childhood I was extremely active in sports including soccer, swimming, and baseball. In high school, I earned 11 varsity letters in these sports and was an all-regional athlete. I was recruited by a number of smaller, Division-1AA colleges but always lacked the size to earn a scholarship at a Division-1 school. When I graduated high school, I was 135 pounds soaking wet!

Deciding to pursue academics over athletics in college, I chose to attend Penn State University Scheyer Honors Program. I graduated as valedictorian with degrees in Biochemistry and Molecular Biology and Economics. Although I was extremely focused on academics, there was something missing. I missed the training involved with athletics so, as a freshman, one of my roommates introduced me to the weight room. I was instantly hooked. Although I lived on cold cereal, by the time I graduated I had a well-built, 175-pound frame and had learned a lot about proper training. After I graduated, my Biochemistry background allowed me to perform my own research and investigation into proper nutrition and supplementation, which really helped me make gains. In 2002, a year after I graduated, I was encouraged by a bodybuilder at my gym to compete. I won the overall novice division at my first show and was instantly hooked. Fourteen months later I won my natural pro card at my second competition and then began competing as a drug-free professional bodybuilder. I've won numerous overall pro titles throughout my career including the Yorton Cup Pro World Championships in 2009 and 2014.

During much of my time as a competitor, I worked as a manager at an economic litigation consulting firm (for 12 years). I started there right after college, about the same time as I picked up bodybuilding competitions as a hobby. Because of my background, I became fascinated with all of the dietary supplements on the market. In reality though, because of my background, I got frustrated (and disgusted) by the horrendous products companies were selling that used under dosed ingredients, fillers, and, my biggest pet peeve, proprietary blends where a company can hide behind very cheap formulas.

I began researching what it would take to bring a product to market that I would want to take. At the time it was a meal replacement. So in 2005, and with a small amount of money, I created our first product, Core MRP, and Core Nutritionals was born. Core Nutritionals is a brand that, to this day, sticks behind the principles of intelligently designed formulas, no fillers, no artificial colors, and no proprietary blends so the consumer can be assured they know exactly what they are consuming.

What started as a hobby turned into career (I quit my day job in 2013). As I became more successful in natural bodybuilding by winning the Pro World Championships a couple of times, the brand took off. Now we are a full line of high quality sports nutrition supplements with almost 100 products that are sold around the world.

The Nutrition Corners also arose out of necessity like Core Nutritionals. Back in 2010 as the Core Nutritionals brand really began to grow, I started seeing that many of the retailers in the supplement industry lacked any real knowledge of what they were actually selling people and were so focused on sales numbers that the customers became nameless and faceless to them. So Stephanie (my wife) and I set out to change that and Arlington Nutrition Corner was born. The idea behind this chain of retail supplement stores was three-fold:

1. We would have the best selection of products (not just pushing a house brand like other large retail chains). We have over 100 brands in our stores (where Core Nutritionals is just one of those brands).

2. Our pricing will be second to none and on par with internet sites (even matching Amazon Prime prices!).

3. And finally, and most importantly, our stores, and more specifically our staff, are there to be a resource (not just a retailer) to our customers. All of our staff truly have a passion for the health and fitness industry and really love what they do. Before they ever sell you a product, they will ask you about your history, your goals, and build that relationship with you. So many people are lost when it comes to how to diet and workout properly, and that is what our stores are there for: to educate and encourage our customers (and then finally to sell them some awesome supplements that will help them achieve their goals). We currently have 10 locations in the Nutrition Corner family.

Our latest ventures include a new supplement line called 'Merica Labz and our new energy drink company called 'Merica Energy. As an owner of retail stores, we have a finger on the pulse of the consumer. People were coming in demanding products that had ridiculous label designs but most of the products were terrible. We thought we could do the over the top marketing better BUT use the same principles of Core to actually make amazing products. We launched 'Merica Labz with our over the top patriotic theme on January 1, 2017 and the response has been nothing short of incredible.

Our brand's marketing celebrates patriotism and how it is open to everyone: regardless of your creed, color, or faith, being a patriot only requires loving America. Given these divisive times, we started a brand to celebrate that. Our products unabashedly, unapologetically, and without reservation or hesitation, celebrate America in all its glory. From the names of our products, to the ad copy, to the labels, to our website, we may as well be shouting "We love America" from a megaphone.

Because of the instant success of this branding, we thought this same marketing would work amazingly well in the energy drink space where new innovation and branding was needed. In May 2018, we launched 'Merica Energy and the industry response has been nothing short of amazing once again. Who knows what we have in store next!?

As someone who worked the corporate grind lifestyle for 12 years (it was a fantastic job). I quickly learned that I needed to do something for a living that I was passionate about; I needed to make it count! This is why I began working 50+ hours a week on top of my normal 50+ hours a week to build these businesses. I wake up every day truly loving my "work." And I truly believe this is one of the keys to making your time on this earth count. If you love your work, you will excel at it, which in turn can influence others to follow their passion and find true happiness in their career.

You have won not one, but two Yorton Cups -- which is the "Mr. Olympia" of natural bodybuilding. How did you stay focused on staying true to your training when the motivation wasn't there?

At the end of the day it is not ever about motivation; it is about discipline. If you can instill discipline in one area of your life, it usually makes it easier to find that discipline in other areas. Soon you begin living a life of discipline. If you are disciplined you can truly accomplish anything, even when there is not motivation. And in fact, I find that the more disciplined you are, the more results come, and the more goals are reached, which can cause you to actually be more motivated, which in turn, makes everything even easier. Your discipline up front can bring you motivation later.

The real question is "how do you instill discipline?" I'm not sure I have the universal answer and I think it is different for everyone. It starts with knowing that disciplined actions equate to "winning." For me it is also my fear of mediocrity and wasting the potential that God has blessed me with.

What are your top three non-negotiables in life? What three things do you do without even thinking twice about them?

1. Having faith in my Lord and Savior Jesus Christ
2. Loving my wife, my kids, and myself unconditionally
3. Uphold high ethics in all areas

You have built one of the world's top nutritional brands with Core Nutritionals. What has been Core's foundational mission that has allowed the brand to continue to grow?

See #3 in question #2 above. We uphold high levels of integrity and ethics in all we do and have created a community of customers, clients, ambassadors, vendors, and employees that do to. We will never waiver from the principles that founded the company many years ago. Many supplement companies offer fantastic promises with little or no information to backup their claims. Others hide behind secret "proprietary" blends, which may contain only trace elements of the advertised ingredients. We don't take shortcuts or skimp on effective ingredients just to save a buck, and we don't use "fillers." Core Nutritionals always lets the consumer know exactly what is in its products, guarantees quality with rigorous testing, and even backs up product claims with blood work results. Also, all Core Nutritional products are manufactured in the U.S. and in cGMP facilities.

What is your favorite quote and why?

Our slogan/Mantra at Core Nutritionals is CRUSH IT®. The Core Nutritionals brand is built on and represented through an everyday adherence to the CRUSH IT® mentality. From the gym to the stage, at home, and in our relationships with colleagues, customers, and industry affiliates, this commitment never waivers. We strive for perfection and success but always remain committed to our unwavering integrity and values while helping to bring out the best in others.

What is the most difficult decision you have had to make?

One of the most difficult decisions I had to make was breaking the golden handcuffs of the corporate world to pursue my passion. I gave up a VERY lucrative job and benefits to go all in with my passion in 2013. The minute I left, though, I never looked back and never questioned my decision.

What piece of advice would you give a younger version of yourself?

This is very much related to the hardest decision I had to make. If I had to do it over again, I would have left my day job 5 years earlier. Now, I don't regret working there because I learned some amazing skills I still use (and are much needed) today and the money allowed me to finance these businesses, but I would have told myself to follow my passion earlier on. I have encouraged numerous people in my same position to "go all in," to "make it count," and pursue their passion over the dollar and not once has the outcome been negative. If you are truly passionate about something, people will see that and you will have no problem being successful.

Who has had the biggest impact on your journey?

I don't think there is one person who has had the biggest impact on my journey. I think it's a combination of the love and support of my parents at a young age, the love and support of my wife now, and the amazing group of passionate team members I have surrounded myself with and have the privilege of working with on a daily basis.
I never really had an entrepreneurial mentor. This is one of the reasons I enjoy working with young entrepreneurs now.

What does the words "Make It Count" mean to you?

To me, MAKE IT COUNT and CRUSH IT are interchangeable. It isn't just a catchy slogan, it's a lifestyle that you live and breathe every day. It's giving it your all in EVERYTHING you do and not just so that things will be better for your own future, but the future of others as well.

CHAPTER 12

Bookends

"Dream as if you'll live forever, live as if you'll die today."

- James Dean

There are two words that come into play when we think about bookends — or should I say, how this chapter relates to living your life within the bookends of today.

Catastrophizing; *worrying about something that hasn't happened yet.*
Ruminating; *worrying about or over-evaluating events that happened in the past.*

As humans, we have a gift for worrying about the future and overthinking things that have already happened. We hold onto events from the past, with the intention to keep rummaging through the possibilities instead of taking them for what they are. They are part of the learning process. And as far as future events, Mark Twain said it best, "I have known a great many troubles but most of them never happened." Living a "Make It Count" lifestyle is being constantly focused on delivering your best each and every day. It's when we deliver that potential each day that our personal stock rises. To be our best requires our best effort. However, when we start becoming anxious about a past or future event, we instantly lose the potential for that moment. Our decisions and thoughts become blinded and we waste the greatness in that moment.

Practicing a method which I like to call the "bookends of today," allows us to focus only on the now. It is a friendly reminder to us that life unfolds in the present. Yesterday is done, so learn from it and move on. Tomorrow is never guaranteed, so why bother allowing destructive thoughts into your perfect, current day. The *art* of bookends is that it sustains life and keeps out the negative. Bookends hold the heaviest, strongest books in place on your shelf. Bookends in your day do the same towards keeping your mind focused on the strongest principles needed to "Make It Count." Nothing gets past the bookend from yesterday, and, sure enough, nothing from tomorrow either. Living within the bookends of today does not mean that you are sheltering yourself from others. It's actually quite the opposite. When we live within the parameters of today, we are allowed to be 100% focused on the here and now. This enormous focus factor allows us to be truly present in our jobs, our relationships, our friendships, our health, and anything else that has meaning to us. We're not being forced to barter with outside thoughts about things we can't change, and instead we can give our undivided attention to the immediate situation.

When I went back to school to pursue my doctorate, after 5 years in the professional world, school seemed so much easier than in my undergrad years. I believe this was mainly because I had matured, but also because I devoted each day to what had to be done — rather than stressing over events that were either completed or had yet to happen. When we live within the bookends of today, we become unaffected by the negative circumstances around us. Instead, we pay more attention to how we can help. In a multiple day mental state, we are simply feeding the monkey mind. Just like a monkey swings from vine to vine, a monkey mind encourages swinging from thought to thought. Practicing the bookend mindset helps train the monkey mind to focus narrowly on what is important — which thoughts are going to maximize today and only today, as anything out of the next *now* is just a possibility.

I know what you must be thinking, "This all sounds great, Jake, but it's impossible to implement. It's impossible not to focus on past events, and how could I ever stop thinking about future events?" Well, I agree with you and know it's not a perfect system — simply installing a fictional set of bookends and moving on with your day. You have to work at it just like anything else, constantly readjusting your bookends to make sure they are set in place to hold up your biggest, strongest and boldest thoughts, actions and principles.

How To Implement The Make It Count Bookends:

1. **Practice gratitude.** — The strongest technique for living in the present is to practice gratitude. Gratitude allows us to focus on what we have, instead of what we don't have. We each have gifts laying around us constantly —whether it's your family, your health, your job, your inspirational neighbor, or even a book you just read. When we sit down each morning and start the day with gratitude, our mindfulness grows toward intentionally living in the path of what we appreciate. Gratitude shows us what is possible if we take a second to identify what is good in our lives. Gratitude also shows us how we can level up our game, if we are present to what means the most to us.

2. **Pick door number three**. — In Alex Banayan's book, *The Third Door,* he talks about what is behind the three doors. He says that the first door is where the line wraps around the block, the second door is for the celebrities and VIP guests, and the third door is completely up to our imagination of what is possible. The third door is the creativity of finding a way into the club, the event, or the situation. Life is no different when we live between the bookends of your day. The third door in our day opens to doing something we have never done before. When we get out of our comfort zone, we focus on the now. We don't worry about what lies outside of the bookends, mainly because we have no time. We are in the moment, curious as to whether this will all work out. We are wondering why the heck we chose this path, and we are trying to process our next steps. All the third door does is allow us to be present on what matters most *right now*. The

now is the powerful equation to what steps we will take today in order to build a better foundation for ourselves.

3.   **Breathe.** — My wife hates it when she is stressed and I tell her to breathe, but, physiologically, focusing on the breath helps to control our state and next move. When we are stressed or frantic, and we don't know what to do next, sometimes the easiest approach we can take is to stop. Take 6 deep breaths, in and out, and reset our direction. Focused breathing has the ability to dial in our heart rate, decrease cortisol (stress hormone) levels, oxygenate the body, and clear distractions from the mind.

4.   **Stop sacrificing health**. — We only get one vessel in this lifetime. There are no upgrades, there aren't many second chances, and our direction is often centered around the energy that our body and mind creates. When we skip meals, seek quick and unhealthy food sources, complain about not having enough time to exercise, and stop the simple meditation practices we use to deal with stress, we are ignoring the foundation of everything we do. That foundation of health is what will make today the most impactful. If we're not feeling alive, full of energy, and willing to fight for what is ours, then we will struggle to crush our goals.

5.   **Stop focusing on just making ends meet.** — Have you ever noticed that when you are not fully focused on your day, that you often do just enough to get to the next meeting, appointment, or project? You don't take the extra step in order to truly find your gift. When we are just going through the motions to make ends meet — or worse, living according to someone else's schedule — then we are not truly enjoying what we have right now. We are not focused on present time perfection, but more on doing just enough to get to tomorrow. Stop doing just enough, and instead raise your level of attendance by going all in on your day. Your work will explode with success, you will leave a lasting mark on more people, and you will truly be able to be more attentive to the moment.

6.   **Flow state**. — This is probably one of my favorite reasons to enjoy the life within the bookends of your day. There are some great books out there on the flow state, including *The Rise of Superman* by Steven Kotler. Enough research has been done to identify what happens when someone enters a state of flow. In a nutshell, it allows us to enter an almost zen state, in which everything flows smoothly and at the pace we desire. This puts us expertly into the moment, which is what living a Make It Count lifestyle is all about. Hobbies are a great example of a potential flow state: something we enjoy, that allows us the gift of living present time

focused. My flow state is always exercise. It checks all the boxes for me in terms of taking care of my health and crushing my goals. But to truly get the most out of a session, I have to be in the moment.

We have to stop letting the present slip away because we are focused on the wrong moment in time. Every chapter, or each day, provides us with the gift of life. That gift is one that is never guaranteed. What *are* guaranteed are the moments that we turn into our memories. However, the only way to capitalize on the moments is to live within the bookends of your day. Ignoring the time caps of yesterday and tomorrow are crucial to our success in this world. A leader leads with the promise that within each second they are living to make both their life and the lives of those around them count.

Make It Count Foundations

1. Do you focus more on the past or on the future? What are three things you can do today, in order to change that?

2. Practicing daily gratitude provides us with a field map of whether or not we are on the right path. What are three things you are grateful for, and why?

3. The monkey mind is a real thing that distracts many people's progress. The next time you notice yourself swinging from thought to thought, grab some paper and unleash those thoughts onto the paper. This helps you train the monkey mind to be more focused, and potentially use those thoughts for your benefit.

4. Mindfulness is a trendy word these days. And it *should* be, as living intentional gives us clarity in our journey. What are three things you will do with intention today?

5. Living within the bookends of you day is not a perfect science. You *will* run into memories of the past that you have trouble dealing with. The goal is to take those memories and ask yourself what you can learn from that moment? How can this memory make you a better person today? We also stress over the future, far more than we should. For example, when you have a big speech coming up and all you can think about is screwing up and not delivering the right message you want to convey, the key to not overthink the future and to maximize the present. Practice the speech in the mirror, practice in front of friends, and recognize that people are going to make judgments. But if your speech comes from a point of passion, then the odds of you crushing the talk are very high. The more you stress about the future, the more you realize that those stresses never happen. Either you crush the goal, or you walk away never fully living up to the potential you had.

Make It Counter: Henry Humm

Hello, my name is Henry Humm. I am 51 years old and live in Ellicott City, MD with my beautiful wife Noelle and our blended family of boys Alex, Matt and Aaron. By day I am a Sales and Marketing Executive within the Health Insurance field. To my friends and family, I am a warrior. You see, I am blessed to be writing this as I am a four-time transplant recipient of two hearts and two kidneys. There is not one day that goes by that I do not thank God for my donors and donor families. My journey began back in 1983 when I was diagnosed with cardiomyopathy and a hole between my ventricles. I was a sophomore in high school and a three-sport athlete. Soccer was my passion as my dad taught me to play. Thankfully, I received my heart transplant on July 12, 1984, from a boy in Michigan, and returned to the soccer field by the end of August about 45 days after my transplant. Things went well for about 10 years until I developed atherosclerosis (hardening of the arteries) from my medications which required me to go back on the transplant list. Thankfully, again the call came, and I received my second gift of life on April 7, 1995. One of the downfalls of organ transplantation is the anti-rejection medications can cause kidney failure. After taking them for 18 years, my kidneys began to fail. I found myself once again on the transplant list-this time for a kidney. I was blessed that my sister Debbie, my angel, stepped up and volunteered to be tested to see if she was a match. Thankfully she was a perfect match and she donated her kidney to me on June 4, 2002. My life returned to normal once again and in August 2013 I met Noelle. Our relationship blossomed and I found myself proposing to her on June 30, 2016, on Smith Island. We immediately started planning our wedding for June 2017, in Kure Beach NC. I have always been active and developed an infection in my knee in early 2017 and by April had surgery to remove an infected bursa. The surgery did not go smoothly, and I became septic afterward. I ended up in the ICU where Noelle had to fight to get me transferred to Johns Hopkins where they were able to stabilize me. I learned then and there not to mess with Noelle. As a result of my knee surgery, my kidneys took another hit and I was told I would need another transplant. I never fully recovered and I was weak and sick for our wedding on June 29, 2017. We returned from our honeymoon and by the end of July, I was starting dialysis. I hate dialysis as it takes so much out of a person, but thankfully, I was only on dialysis for about two months when Noelle and I received the call that a kidney was available. We just looked at each other cried and prayed for the donor family. On September 23, 2018, I received the gift of life for a fourth time: a kidney. My life has never been easy, but I would not have it any other way because it has made me the man I am today. Through all of this, I have always been able to keep a positive attitude and never give up. I am a member of Team Maryland and compete in the Transplant Games every other year. I have attended 7 transplant games and won multiple medals in track & field, tennis, and volleyball. Hopefully, Noelle and I will be traveling to Newcastle Gateshead UK in August 2019 to compete in the World Transplant Games. A good friend always tells me to "keep on keeping on" and that's just what I do. One day at a time, one moment at a time, with the love of my life by my side, I will continue to fight for every day I have on this earth always paying homage to my donors, donor families, and my sister.

I feel like, one day, there should be a whole book dedicated to your life's journey. You have been through so much, and most people would have given up long ago. How have you fought through the obstacles with such tenacity, while also having an endless stream of positive energy?

I have always said God has a plan for me. God only challenges those he knows can handle it. Many people over the years say I'm the strongest person they know. I always thank them and accept the compliment but really that person is God.

What is your favorite quote and why?

I have to say it's by Winston Churchill and it's quite simple. "Never, Never, Never give up", I have not and never will.

Life has thrown you multiple curve balls, yet your focus is unwavering. What habits, tools or tactics do you have in place that have led to a continuous growth mindset?

First and foremost, I'm a Christian and try to always do what's right. Church with my family is a big part. Noelle & I love going to the church with the boys. I'm a member of Team Maryland and whenever I can, I help promote Organ Donations. Lastly, laugh! I truly believe that laughter keeps me going.

Each year you participate in the Transplant Games. What positive lifestyle metric have you learned surrounding yourself with such inspirational people?

Wow, where to start. Each and every one of us at the Games is here today because of someone's else's unselfish gift. We all try to honor our donors and live our life to the fullest. The friends and families we meet are what is all about. It's not about the medals, it's about the camaraderie.

What one thing has made the biggest impact on your life?

My family. I am extremely close to my family. My parents, sisters, nieces, nephew are always behind me. My beautiful wife, Noelle, and my boys, Alex & Aaron, keep me fighting every day to be here.

What piece of advice would you give to a younger version of yourself?

Always have a positive attitude. No matter how bad it looks or sounds, be positive. You can do it.

We all reach stages in our life where we feel overwhelmed. What do you do when you feel overwhelmed?

Exercise. I work out about 4-5 days a week on average and not only does it relieve my stress it puts my mind at ease.

I believe you're the mascot for what it means to "Make It Count!" What does "Make It Count" mean to you?

I'd have to say be humble, do your best, and help others. I think if everyone was like this the world would be a better place to live.

CHAPTER 13

Stronger Than Your Strongest Excuse

"Attitude not aptitude determines your altitude."

- Zig Ziglar

What do you fight most for each day? Do you fight for the life you want? Or do you find yourself fighting to defend your excuses and limitations?

The answer for most people is that they are fighting to defend the excuses more than the life they really want. Excuses allow us to rationalize the dozen plus reasons why we can't do something. They give us an immediate reason why something cannot or will not work out. Excuses are not, nor will they ever be, grounded in success. That is, until you wake up and realize that you are basing your actions and responses on those excuses. When we finally come to the conclusion that in order to design the lifestyle we want, we first need to come to terms with our excuses, then we can go ahead and build something special.

Success occurs when your dreams get bigger than your excuses. Success occurs when you build up your physical and mental strength to be ready for battle against your strongest excuse. The first step is to realize what excuses actually are. According to *Mirriam-Webster*, the word can be defined as any of the following:

1. To make apology for
2. To try to remove blame from
3. To forgive entirely or disregard as a trivial import
4. To grant exemption or release to
5. To allow to leave
6. To serve as an excuse for

As you can see, the common theme within these definitions is to give yourself an out and not be associated with the outcome. The problem is that we are usually seeking an out on our dreams, our health, and on the presence of those around us for years to come.

Next, we have all heard and used the most common excuses at some point in our lifetimes: that there's not enough time, not enough money, not enough connections, or having kids makes it too difficult. Or maybe our excuses are that we don't have enough talent, we're too old, we're overweight, we're too tall or too short, we're not smart enough, we weren't raised in the right setting, we don't belong to a gym, or we're stuck in the job we have at the moment. These are just a sampling of the excuses we use on a daily basis. When we use these excuses, we allow our negative mind to take over our dreams and goals. We experience a short window of what feels like relief, but essentially what we are doing is closing the larger window to life. Excuses only cause regret; they hold us back, limit growth potential, stop challenging us, and stop allowing us to grow into the people we were meant to be.

It's also funny to me the kinds of people who use excuses in their lives. People who have been through tough times are typically the ones who learn to ignore excuses, and they treat them like the waste of time and energy that they are. It's the rest of us who go through life minimally challenged, with lofty goals and dreams, who rely on excuses and let them define us. We spend time on social media, daydreaming about the lives of others, yet we make the excuse that those people are just "gifted." Those people are unique and have talents that we could never dream of. Comparison becomes our excuse — that life would be great if we could just have what that other person has.

I am here to tell you that you do indeed have everything that the other person has — and more! You just need to be stronger than your strongest excuse. You need to develop the principles that will take you to your dream life. That life is waiting for you, once you realize that you are holding yourself back. Henry Humm, our Make It Counter from the previous chapter, has every reason in the world to excuse himself from living the life he wants. From cancer, to organ failure, to an organ transplant, this man has been through the gamut of life crises. He has first hand experience that says that life can be unfair at times. However, he chose to ignore the option of using these unfortunate events as excuses. He now lives the life he wants because he has made the choice to persevere during difficult times. He understands the fragility of life. And when one comes to terms with how fragile life is, then one can also realize the wasted effort that excuses truly are.

In the "Make It Count" mindset, we strategize excuses in accordance to our goals. Categorizing goals, or actionable steps, into **should vs. must** helps us create a pathway to break down our excuses. This helps us to create the journey we need. When our goals are centered around the idea that we *should* meet them, then we often rationalize ways out of our actions. *Should's* are not strong enough, as there is no solid foundation behind them. A great example would be saying, "I should stop eating these french fries, but they are too good. I can always stop tomorrow." But when a goal is a *must*, then there is no other option than to carry out the goal. The word *must* creates a foundation for change. It leaves nothing open for having a secondary option. It creates an energy within us that drives change. Following our example, we might say, "I must stop eating these fries, because my health is important to me and my health will allow me to be there for my kids for decades to come."

Should's are weak by nature, and they don't force change. Whereas *must's* create the inertia to make a difference right now! Continuously feeding our excuses allows them to define us. When they define us, we lose the power to become the "game changers" we were meant to be. So, why do we make excuses? We make excuses out of fear, failure, uncertainty, comparison, protection, and a lack of goals. They help us to rationalize our way out of something. How do we change our excuses and become a stronger version of ourselves? Everything revolves around action and mindset. If someone were to read this chapter and just expect change, then that person would be waiting for a long time. When our mindset is set to positive thinking, and that positive thinking inspires action, then the fuel for change increases and we lose the energy needed to make excuses.

5 Steps to Being Stronger Than Your Strongest Excuse

1. **Stop Comparing** — The phenomenon of comparing your life to another is not a new idea; it has been going on for as long as humans have been alive. What is new is the percent of people who are living their whole lives in comparison. The problem with comparison is that, the majority of the time, it's very unhealthy. Healthy comparison consists of tactics as displayed in the "Steal The Mirror" chapter. When you can compare to someone else's success, and find what they are doing right, you can learn how to implement those strategies into your life for positive change. Comparison becomes dangerous when you see other people's success — their material items, their six pack abs, their new jobs, or their luxury trips — and you start the "Why not me?" process. You see how perfect someone's life seems on social media, and you immediately get frustrated because your life doesn't look that way. Then, instead of taking the right path and integrating positive change towards the dream you would like to live, you start with excuses as to why you can't have that life. So, growth mindset number one is to stop comparing apples to oranges. Your life is *your* life, and you are the captain of your ship. You can have anything you want in life if you take the first step and stop comparing yourself to others. Comparison leads to chasing the wrong metrics, and, at the first sign of stress, the captain of that ship usually jumps overboard.

2. **Stop Blaming** — Think of the great leaders in your life, whether that's your boss, a coach you had, or that uncle you love. Have you ever heard them blame someone else for their own hard times or failures? Have you ever heard them use someone else as their excuse? My guess is that this has never happened. Great leaders don't blame others for a mishap. They take full responsibility and they learn from the event instead. Sure, someone in their circle could be responsible for losing an account, but the leader takes ownership and acknowledges they should have done a better job teaching the steps. Blaming others is an excuse that won't lead to anything positive. When we blame others, we don't take ownership of the situation. This tends to lead to repetitive negative events. Also, when we blame others, we are not reinforcing the process of

teamwork and community. We push ourselves into a corner where no one wants to listen to what we have to say in the future.

3. **Age is Never a Limit** — We live in a time when age is an excuse of the past. I have seen 80-year-olds crush Ironman Triathlons, and I have seen 5-year-olds get a standing ovation for a musical performance. When we place an age restriction on pursuing a goal, we are saying that we are not good enough or that we don't have the right passion to keep going. Not having the passion is fine, but don't use age as your "way out."

4. **Take Action** — The only thing that trumps action, is not taking action. The second you take action on a goal, your excuses become smaller and smaller. You might not meet your goal today, but you will sure be closer to it than you were yesterday. Action doesn't have time for excuses. As a doctor who preaches health and wellness through exercise, I hear people everyday telling me that they don't have time for exercise. My responses vary: "You will have time for health issues later in life," or "You have time to limit social media to only 30 minutes a day," or "You had time to come see me, when exercise would have fixed this," or "It doesn't take much to wake up earlier and go for a 20-30 minute walk." When the right priorities are put in place, we suddenly have tons of free time. Health and wellness take a little effort in the beginning, but their positive impact will make you forget about the time excuse really fast. It becomes habit, and habits are strong. And habits always begin with taking action.

5. **Learn** — When we expand our knowledge, we begin expanding our opportunities. Last year, you may have had an excuse for not being able to pursue a certain job. But if you're expanding your learning base, why shouldn't you be able to pursue that job? Books, seminars, videos, and mentors allow you to consistently up your learning game. These avenues allow you to increase your passion awareness and always be thirsty for more knowledge. It's that knowledge, combined with the principles learned in this book, that will crush any and all excuses that sneak onto your plate.

In the end, strength doesn't come from muscles. Strength doesn't come from one action, and strength doesn't come from just saying you will do something. Strength comes from consistent habits, done over and over again. These habits turn into subconscious actions on your behalf. Things that you do without thinking. You program exercise because it feels right. You make the cold calls at work because it's who you are.

You don't quit on the lifestyle eating challenge that you have taken on because you know how it will turn your health around.

Make It Count Foundations

1. What is the biggest excuse that you use on a consistent basis? Focus on incorporating one thing that you can do consistently over the next week, to make that excuse disappear.

2. Look at your goals. Are they **should's or must's**? How can you change your goals, so that they become stronger and allow you a stronger relationship with success?

3. One day challenge! Try to go one day without blaming anyone else for things not working out. Stop using other people as an excuse and start taking ownership for everything you do. When we take ownership, we learn how to be better for everyone in our circle.

4. What is your biggest weakness? When we make excuses, we are feeding our weaknesses instead of starving them. We are consciously telling ourselves that these weaknesses are okay, and that the effort to course correct the weakness is not worth our time. Identify three weaknesses in your life and, for one week, develop habits to work on those weaknesses. When we starve the weakness of excuses, the excuses die off never to return.

5. Consistency is the basis for all positive progression. When you are consistent with your new growth habits, you will ignore the excuses. Stay consistent, no matter the obstacles, and your excuses will have no foundation within you.

Make It Counter: Janine Kirkland

I grew up in a small town in Illinois where everyone knew each other. At the age of 21, I married my high school sweetheart. When I was 22, I gave birth to Jacob, my son, and three years later gave birth to twin girls. Life had its ups and downs but overall everything seemed good. When the twins were seven, one of them became seriously ill and spent several weeks at the Children's hospital in Chicago. Two months after we came home from the hospital my husband decided that he didn't want to live with us anymore and left. My whole life was suddenly turned upside down. I had a great support group of family and friends that helped me get my life back on track. I had to work several jobs to make ends meet and I had three children to take care of. I didn't have time to feel sorry for myself.

In the long run, it turned out that my husband leaving us was the beginning of a new, better life. Six months later, I met a wonderful, caring man. He had four children from another marriage, and I had three, which meant that we had seven children between us. A year later we were married and began our journey of raising seven children. There were a lot of challenges in blending two families. Three years later, I gave birth to a little girl and our family grew to eight children. When she was six, my husband and I became foster parents and took in an eight-year-old girl. Two years later, we adopted her, and our family grew once again.

My husband and I believed in giving back to our community. For 20 years, my full-time job was volenterring. I have had the opportunity to volunteer and work with numerous agencies and non-profit organizations. I learned and grew as a person from each experience. I am now retired. My husband and I live in Mexico in a small Mexican village in the mountains. I still volunteer and still try to MAKE EVERY DAY COUNT!

You have volunteered for numerous boards over your lifetime. What has been the most fulfilling role and why?

I have had the opportunity to volunteer and work with numerous agencies and non-profit organizations over the years. I learned and grew as a person from each experience. It would be hard to choose one that I liked the best because they were all so different. I would say that I always enjoyed volunteering where it would benefit my children such as their schools or where I could work with them such as scouting, coaching cheerleading or producing shows for Children's Theatre of Elgin. It always meant a lot to me to be involved in their lives.

Since moving to Mexico, my most fulfilling volunteer project is working with Operation Feed in San Juan Cosala which is one of the poorest villages in our area. I started a project called "Ladies of San Juan Cosala." I work with seven unbelievable women who have taught me so much about life. Through this project these women are learning new productive skills, building self-confidence and a sense of self-worth and making money to help support their families. These women live in houses with dirt floors and no windows. They don't have a stove and cook on an open fire pit in their backyard. They have taught me that material things don't make you happy. Family and friends and your outlook on life make you happy. They brighten my day every time I see them. THEY MAKE EVERY DAY COUNT!

At one point in your life, you worked numerous jobs to make sure that your three kids had clothes on their back, food on the table, and the perks that life has to offer. What was your driving force behind these actions?

I think that good parents always put the needs and well being of their children first. At the time I never really thought about working numerous jobs. I just did what was necessary to be a single mom and to make ends meet. I also had great support from family and friends. When I needed help there was always someone there to help me. At that time in my life I had to MAKE IT COUNT every day for the needs and well being of my three children.

You have crushed many goals in your lifetime, such as going back to college in your 50's. Why did you go back to school when you didn't need to, and what did you learn about yourself?

When I turned 50 I decided to go back to college. My youngest daughter was in middle school and I felt that it was time to do something for myself. I enrolled in our community college for Graphic Design. It was very intimidating going back to school with people half my age. Plus they were all knowledgeable on the computer and I barely knew how to turn it on. My teachers were all my age and were extremely supportive and helpful. The young people in my classes were also very supportive, understanding and they taught me a lot. I learned to believe in myself and work hard. It took me four years to finish and I never got a grade below an A. If I was going to take the time to go back to school I knew that I had TO MAKE IT COUNT!

What do the words "Make it Count" mean to you?

I have learned to never ask why should I do that or why should I help that person and always ask why wouldn't I do that and why wouldn't I help that person? The happiness and joy that I get from helping people in need is so great. It touches my heart and makes me a better person. That is what the words MAKE IT COUNT means to me.

What piece of advice would you give a younger version of yourself?

The best thing that ever happened to me was the day when my first husband left me. It made me look at life differently and become my own person. I feel that I became the person that I was meant to be. I no longer had to be afraid to voice my opinion or do something that would upset him. I was free to be me. So my advice would be to always be yourself and never end up in a relationship where you cannot be yourself and have to become a person someone else wants you to be. Always being yourself is the best way to MAKE IT COUNT!

In a roundabout way, you have helped raise 9 kids. What one lesson have you learned from being a parental leader to different personalities?

I have learned that no two children are the same. They are all individuals. I have identical twins and they are as different as night and day. I have an awesome husband and between the two of us we always tried to work out every problem together. Our two youngest daughters probably had it the toughest as we learned a lot from our mistakes with the older children and did not repeat our mistakes with them. We always said that GOD gives every family a child that is challenging, however when you have nine children you end up with two or three that challenge you. I will not mention any names because they know who they are. My husband believes in creating good memories for children and family vacations was big on his list. Every year we went on a big vacation and took all the children that were able to go with, us. Creating memories is also a great way to MAKE IT COUNT!

You have been my hero my entire life. What do parents need to do more often to make sure that they are making their time count with their kids?

I think that parents just need to be involved in their children's lives. To attend all of the sporting events, school events, etc. and let them know that you care about them and what they do. We always tried to have dinner together as a family every night. It is a great way to ask everyone about their day and get to know what is important to them and going on in their lives. One time we had a good friend join us for dinner and at the end of dinner he said, "I don't know how you can listen to three or four people talk at the same time". I told him, "You get used to it". Spending time with your children and having dinner together is a great way to MAKE IT COUNT!

What is one piece of advice that your parents taught you, that you have carried with you your entire life?

I grew up in a small community in which my parents were very involved. The year that I was born my dad founded a Lions Club in our town. He worked hard to raise enough money to build a clubhouse and was the first president. To this day the Lions Club is one of the main social and charitable institution in our town. When I was eight-years-old, I held a fundraiser in my neighborhood and donated the money to the Lions Club. So from a young age I was taught to give back to my community and to help the people that are less fortunate and need my help. I have been doing that since then. Helping people and giving back is a great way to MAKE IT COUNT.

CHAPTER 14

*Happens **for** You and Not **to** You*

*"It's not what happens to you, but how you react
to it that matters."*

- Epictetus

One of the biggest lessons I have learned — and continue to learn over time — is that I am not a victim of life. Most of us approach life with a "Why me?" mentality, instead of asking "Why not me?" The biggest change we can make is to stop thinking that life is happening *to* us. Life is just life and, not to hurt your feelings, but life doesn't care about you, or me, or anyone else. Life is just a boulder rolling down the mountain, until there is no more mountainside for it to traverse. As the boulder rolls, things will happen. Greatness will develop and rough times will serve us. It's *how* we view what happens along the path of the boulder, that determines the type of life we will live. Life is a blessing waiting for us to accept that simple fact. Life is meant to be lived by looking at each opportunity or situation through the lens of life's actions happening *for* us.

For most of my life, I have dealt with a dad who enjoyed the bottle more than he enjoyed engaging in moments to make memories. As a boy, and then young man, I wanted to look up to my dad as a hero and as someone to give me guidance. I felt constantly disappointed in our journey together. Until recently — as it took many years for me to understand — I always felt that the situation of having a parent with a lifelong addiction was not fair. I thought that having a parent with an addiction, stronger than his love for his kids, was life kicking me in the face. But all of this changed when I decided to change my perspective. All of the emotions, that I had been bottling up for so many years, changed when I realized that I was fighting someone that I couldn't control.

I never gave up on supporting my dad; I had him writing his goals to me everyday for years, and I saw reaching out as the only form of therapy I could offer. The most powerful thing happened when I realized that having an absent dad — self-focused on alcohol, and not willing to change — was only an avenue for making me a better person, and especially a better father. This chapter in life was meant to show me how to be the best dad that I could be. This experience was meant to make me enjoy the laughs, to understand that having kids is a gift, and to realize that being a dad is not something to be taken for granted.

When we realize that life entails the good, the bad, the sad, the disappointed, the success, the failure, the growth and *all* events in between, then we can grow through everything that happens in our lives. When we understand that no matter how much we try to control, that everything will shift and change — that it's up to us to perceive what the event or emotion means to us — then we can fight like we've never fought before to own our reactions for positive growth.

There is a great quote by Byron Katie, on the simplicity of life happening *for* us and not *to* us:

" Life is simple. Everything happens for you, not to you. Everything happens at exactly the right moment, neither too soon nor too late. You don't have to like it...it's just easier if you do."

The key word here is "**easier**."

I'm not saying that getting a cancer diagnosis or hearing that a friend passed away is supposed to be easy. These are both extremely difficult events in life. However, most items that people stress over don't involve life or death situations. People fight life on the simplest of challenges. They don't like their health, their job, their commute, how they're treated, the weather, their lack of motivation, lack of intelligence, their looks, their position in life, their neighbors, the idea of failure, having to work hard — the list goes on forever. When we shift our outlook to see that it's easier to accept and enjoy the challenge of everything happening *for* us, then we stop wasting precious time fighting the things that bother us. We come to the daily conclusion that these things will exist, and we instead learn how to use them to our advantage for better times ahead. All of the "don't likes" listed above just need a cognitive shift in our perception. The acceptance that things *will* happen is first, followed by the perception of what we will do in response.

As I've gotten older, I've found an increase in the number of people I know who have lost a close friend or learn they have been diagnosed with cancer. Death is the most unfortunate event of the gift of life in this world. Death is the only thing that is certain in all our lives. That's why it's so incredibly important to "Make It Count" and live life to its fullest. A friend of mine lost their son recently, and I am sure the grieving process will be long and it will be hard to overcome. The outpouring of love, support, and stories have bought a tear to my eye each time I've read another letter. The amount of positive growth mindset work that this kid did in his 20 years is something most of us will never achieve in an entire lifetime. The kindness, passion, humility, and love that this 20-year-old had during his life — even through his time battling cancer — is inspiring. So, while it will never make sense to lose someone so impactful so young, there is meaning to why he was put on this earth. His life happened for a reason: for us to believe that there is good in people and that no matter how long this journey is, we should make a difference every chance we get. We shouldn't sit by complaining about the little things that are out of our control.

In the psychology world, there is a term called "cognitive reappraisal." In this, we learn how to reframe our thoughts and explore our own reactions. Everything we do should be through the process of cognitive reappraisal; constantly evaluating the meaning of each situation. Constantly throwing away the garbage, and only allowing that which is beneficial to us into our mindset. Constantly adjusting to an environment of learning.

Cognitive reappraisal involves restructuring your emotional response to what is going on around you.

When I was in the thick of triathlon racing, I had a string of three races where mechanically I broke down, physically I feel apart and my times put me towards the back of the pack, that I started to fall apart emotionally. I realized that there were bigger problems to stress over, but when you put so many hours into something and it doesn't work out, it takes a very strong armor to keep those emotions away. I would train harder after each failure, only to have a bad race again. One day, I decided to forgo my daily training and take inventory of what was happening instead. What I came to realize was that my training was perfect but my perception of myself as a competitive triathlete was flawed. I had emotionally lost faith in myself — but only on race day. At that time, I performed a cognitive reappraisal of what was going on and I dumped the garbage emotions that were blocking me from success.

Guess what happened the next race?

I won the whole triathlon!

Looking back on this, I can see that it was 100% happening *for* me. I was not accepting that in order to perform your best in any event, you need to be connected to your mind and body. It's not as simple as just going through the emotions, but it is also taking inventory of your emotional response to everything you do. Sometimes the emotional response, or action, is stronger than just a simple switch. In this case, the best thing you can do is just perceive that its beneficial. You don't have to fully believe that your choice will help. But if you perceive the challenge to be beneficial or to have a positive influence on your life, then the next step comes at the right time. If your ability to explore your reaction to life involves just the continuous perception that everything happens for a reason, then as you progress you confirm *why* as you go.

A couple of years ago, I was let go from a job I loved. This initial blow was difficult to swallow; I had never been fired from a job before. And on top of that, a non-compete clause would limit my ability to practice for an entire year. For about two months, I struggled. Then I started to realize all of the avenues that were opening up to me that would never have happened if I hadn't gotten fired. I started to believe that life was happening *for* me: that all this was meant to be, and that it was up to me to make the most out of my action. I not only got to spend more quality time with my kids, but I also traveled more. I became an ambassador to a worldwide brand that has opened too many doors to count. I suddenly had time for friends that I hadn't had time for before. I started taking actions on my dreams in life, and I landed my feet in another practice that has grown my bandwidth more than before. It was a reminder that nothing is forever.

When we come to terms with the fact that nothing is forever, we can almost immediately take pride in the now. All of our power lies in the now. All of our power lies in the belief that everything happens for a reason. All of our power is born through the belief that we are indeed powerful in our actions.

"Happen to things, don't let things happen to you." - Stephen Covey

Make It Count Foundations

1. Start your day with a growth mindset. Shift perspective from "Why me?" to "Why not me?"

2. Don't fight life and don't fight yourself for what you can't control.

3. Reach the conclusion that everything in life will happen regardless if you are ready or not. The good, the bad, and the ugly *will* take a step into your life at some point during your journey. When we accept that things will happen, we can accept that everything comes to help you grow.

4. Everything happens at the right moment in life. Think about 5 things that have had a positive impact on your life, and 5 things that have had a negative impact on your life. All ten items are sure to have inspired growth when you identify the next steps you took.

5. Explore your reaction to all emotions within your day. If things seem off, then take a 5 minute break. Take a cognitive reappraisal of what is going on and then, based on what happens next, make adjustments.

Make It Counter: Filiz McNamara

My name is Filiz Kayagil McNamara. I am a native of Turkey and have been living in America for the past 15 years. Growing up in Turkey, in a very modest household with my brother and sister, we learned how to live on very little, working hard for what we had and taking care of it. I was able to finish my undergraduate degree in Fine Art Education Major in Graphic Design, then I was swept off my feet by my American husband and we moved to the U.S. Thinking I would become a graphic designer, I obtained my master's degree in business in hopes of starting my own company. I did open two LLC's, but neither of them were focused on graphic design. Shortly after I finished my master's degree, I fell in love with personal training and haven't looked back! It is in fitness that I have been able to find the best version of myself, discovered the strength in people, and have been able to develop my passion. Currently I run a team of coaches and trainers with Herbalife Nutrition, it gives me purpose, freedom, and personal development that I cherish!

What does your perfect day look like?

If you had asked me this question 5 years ago, I would have answered much differently than today! The sun gives me so much energy and power for my day; I am all about emotion, attitude, and feelings, the weather plays an important role in my day! I am very blessed and passionate about my job and my team. When I see progress and positive message for the day, my entire day gets better! Wellness is a big part of my life, it is one key area that I have personally suffered through and I would not want anyone to experience such a journey! When I get simple message from a friend, client or family member saying, "Thank you Filiz", I do feel really good. I never thought I would feel this way again… it's my perfect day!

What is your greatest failure and what lesson did you learn from it?

Patience is my great failure. From time to time I try to remind myself to slow down and to stick with the plan. I have been tested many, I mean many, times with this area! When moving to the US from Turkey, it was a great honor to have the opportunity to travel and build better success in US. I was very focused and dedicated to my mission! I wanted to make sure I could further my education and be the best at whatever I chose to do. Not everything went the way we planned after we moved. Being a military spouse you have to act quick or before you know it, you are being left behind. In the 16 years with my husband and the Air Force I have moved 9 times, been through three floods, miscarried several times, separated from my husband, became isolated from my family, lost our son Armand, and had to leave him behind and keep moving forward. There has always been a challenge to overcome, a change in plans, difficult decisions to make. The last flood I was in, as I watched the forceful water, I said to myself, "God you love me don't you?" I will learn about patience, and God will be proud of me! Through all of the heartache and challenges, I was able to have little successes that kept me moving forward. Being able to progress in the wake of misfortune had developed my willpower tremendously...still working on the patience part!

You coach, mentor, inspire, and guide individuals all across the world. What has been your driving force behind helping others succeed?

I can credit 2 leaders for this: Zuzana Majorova and Jennifer Micheli. It was my 3rd miscarriage and I was so upset, I remember the day clearly. I feel so sorry for you she (the nurse) said, It felt like time had stopped and my heart in that moment felt like nothing made any sense. I chose to move out of my country, yet I was so sad that I didn't have my family! After the miscarriage I got cleared from doctors to exercise again, I remember going to a spin class and pedaling as fast as I could as if someone was trying to catch me! When I got home I searched for High Intensity Interval Classes, and Zuzana Majorova (Zuzka Light) from Russia found me. She was exercising from her tiny living room with an extreme light hitting her face… Her sweat and her eyes locked me in, I thought, "just do whatever she is doing!" She was real and it looked like she could hurt me, sadly the mindset I was in felt like I wanted more pain. I dedicated myself to complete her program and with great results starting teaching others in my own fitness place.

The second person, Jennifer Micheli is a Herbalife Wellness Coach and Mentor, mom of 3, fitness model, and entrepreneur. She was speaking at an event I went to in a stadium of 30K people. She walked on the stage with strong steps, tall and gracefully. They had her story on the screen how she was so skinny and sick how she become the person who she is today! Her words felt like they were pulling each trouble in my life out of my chest; shame, weakness and problems! It was almost embarrassing but so powerful at the same time. The growth and change she went through showed me I could be that person and help others. Shy, scared, and weak I realized I too could change! I wanted to be her and wanted to be inspiration and motivation to others. I cannot thank her enough!!! I did get a chance to meet with her, hold her hand and said, "You have no idea, how you pulled me out of sticky scary mud, thank you who you are and helping others to be strong!"

Your passion runs deep with being the best version of yourself -- physically, mentally, and spiritually. Where does this passion come from, and how do you maintain that passion each day?

Finding balance is the approach I take to the way I live and try to help others live. In any situation I take a look at where I am mentally, physically, and spiritually. I know that I will always be stronger in one area than another, or the situation may dictate that I be stronger on one area; whatever the case may be this approach allows me the best opportunity to affect my given circumstance.

Respect is another aspect of how I approach daily interaction with anything. We learned it when we were three years old, but somehow it gets lost in the daily grind: the golden rule, "Do unto others as you would have others do unto you." It is timeless and works remarkably well. Finally, being decisive is at the core of everything that I do. No one will get it right 100% of the time, but you have to take all your experience and apply it toward making a decision. Once you have decided, commit and learn from whatever happens next!

What values growing up in Turkey do you think have helped you become the accomplished person you are today?

Turkey is such a beautiful country, rich in culture, history, and, most importantly, family! Growing up there I was very close to all of my extended family, we all lived relatively close to each other and had great relationships. We were exposed to a lot growing up; my father worked 12 hour days six days a week. It wasn't until he was 50 years old that he bought his first car. My Mom worked beside him many days and then had the time to raise the kids, feed everyone, and keep the extended family close!

They had the foresight to prepare my sister, brother, and I for school then made sure we followed through. They knew we had the talent and worked hard to provide us a way. We never had much money growing up, but we always had enough and knew hard work would get us through.

Getting an education in Turkey is not easy, either. Classrooms are crowded, have strict entry requirements, and lots of competition...it's easy to get lost in the mix and just fade away into being average. Because there is so much to overcome I naturally had to work 3 times harder to be successful. I couldn't always outsmart so I had to outwork! I have to say even though we hated the time we had with our extra overload limited access to many things is the best time ever I remember!

I believe these limited access, hard work and many times failing does give me more character who I am today! Don't get me wrong I am very competitive, stubborn as well and learned so much how to control that with Joe!

If you could give advice to a younger version of yourself what would you tell that person?

Stop hiding and get out! Live the life that has been given to you, you are miracle and you are here to test yourself, learn, and become the person you are meant to be! This question does make me feel and see my lost/empty years and it hurts! The word regret originates from mourning the dead, so life and regret cannot coexist...either you choose to live or you let regret consume your existence. Choose life, there is beauty in it.

If I gave you a billboard, and asked you to write your favorite saying, quote, or mantra on it, what would that look like?

I would have lots of green and blue with a big bright sun! Nature is very inspiring to me, there are so many photos of nature that are a reminder of the simplicity of power of life. Once I have my background, there would be an awesome quote from Jim Rohn, Rumi or Wayne Dyer...

"If you really want to do something, you will find a way. If you don't, you will find an excuse." Jim Rohn

"For things to change, You have to change. For things to get better, you have to get better. For things to improve, you have to improve. When you grow, everything in your life grows with you." Jim Rohn

"You don't need to be better than anyone else, you just need to be better than you used to be." Wayne Dyer

"Whatever lifts the corners of your mouth, trust that. " Rumi

I can write more of them but these bring me back to center and remind me where I want to be.

I have always looked up to you as someone who exemplifies what it means to "Make It Count." What does the words "Make It Count" mean to you?

My job is to help as many people as I can reach a goal and help them accomplish whatever challenge they are facing at the moment! Talk about being passionate and enjoying what I do, I'm kind of in love with all of the trouble, difficulties, and growth behind the scenes. No matter what, I will stay on this course because it gives me perspective of life's little challenges. I will make it count for each reason and each person...this is growth!

CHAPTER 15

Passion Is What Makes Your Heart Sing

"Being the richest man in the cemetery doesn't matter to me. Going to bed at night saying, I've done something wonderful. That's what matters."

- Steve Jobs

Imagine it's the first morning after you've finished a self-improvement seminar you'd been wanting to attend for months. You wake up filled with motivation to be better, to do better and to change the world — or at least, to change your world. The first day goes exactly how you would have expected; you're feeling like a brand new person. This continues for a couple of days, but each day you have less and less motivation. Then, about a week later, you wake up and the motivation is gone. You fall back into your old way of doing things. The new habits never took hold into your paradigms of action. That "be better, do better, change the world" motivation has somehow escaped your life.

What happened?

You were relying on motivation to get the job done for you. This is the problem with only being motivated: that motivation is never there when you need it. We ride its coat tails for a few days and then, BOOM, just like that we seem to have lost our mojo for motivation. This is when *passion* comes into play. Passion is stronger than motivation. If you had attended that seminar and developed passion around a concept, or if you had attended the seminar knowing you had a passion brewing for change, then the roots of passion would have been planted deeper into your subconscious. Then, when you woke up feeling unmotivated, you could have tapped into your passion to push you to do the things you needed to but didn't want to do.

So, the age old question is: *How do you develop passion?*

First of all, you need to have some direction. What is it that you want to accomplish? What is it that you want to do in life? What wakes you up early at times because you can't stop thinking about it? What do you like talking to your friends and family about, more than anything else? The answers to these questions are just the start to understanding what you are passionate about. Write down the answers, and then take the most important step toward developing your passion — TAKE ACTION! Passion involves taking action, 100% of the time. When we sit around, pondering what we are going to do, we often ponder ourselves right out of taking action. And so, we continue to sit on the fence.

Entrepreneurship has been a hot word for the last 5-8 years. The great thing about being an entrepreneur is that everything you do is about experimentation: it allows you to find what you are passionate about, through trial and error. You may set up a company selling yellow hats, only to realize that red hats are actually your thing. The only way to know this is through action.

When I was about 8-years-old, I was in love with hats myself. I wanted to develop a hat collection that rivaled those of everyone I knew. Yes, some of my friends had massive shoe collections, but collecting shoes was easy then. Collecting different hats, with different meanings, was going to be "my calling." Sounds easy, right? Well, in 1984, there weren't hat stores at the mall. Options to find hats were few and far between. But, looking back, I didn't know the difference. I set out to visit different businesses, sporting teams, fishing events, festivals, and any place I imagined might carry a hat. In hindsight, my passion wasn't in finding specific hats, but in wanting to do something different. I wanted to have a different identity than my friends. I wanted to have variety in my bedroom, which showed all the pathways I traveled. And mostly, I believe I wanted to set out to prove that at 8 years old, I could make even my craziest ideas happen. Over a year, I think I collected well over 300 hats of different varieties.

If you wait for passion to express itself in your life, you may be waiting for a while. Passion doesn't arrive while waiting for inspiration to strike. You uncover passion through hard work. Hard, meaningful work helps you tap into the meaning of passion in *your* life. Hard work allows you to find out what exactly makes your heart sing. When we are young, we have a variety of jobs — odd jobs that we think are just for earning some extra spending money. In reality, I believe these jobs are put in place to help us identify what we are most passionate about.

When I was in college, I worked for three summers as a mover. We worked 70 to 80 back-breaking hours, each and every week, all summer long. Could I have found an easier job? Of course! However, the hard work was attractive, as it helped us define what we needed to have in order to survive the future. It showed us that we could work extremely hard, make good money, and find meaning in our days. But most importantly, it showed us that working hard had to be the foundation of every job we would take in the future. Even though the work might not have been as physically difficult, it didn't mean we didn't have to bust our hump each and every day we showed up.

Gary Vaynerchuk notably said, "Skills are cheap, passion is priceless."

Whether it was when I was a mover, when I worked as an aspiring sports agent in New York City, or when I am giving a keynote speech or as a chiropractor these days — at the end of the day, everything required some learnable skills. The options to learn at an accelerated rate are staggering these days. What is not staggering is combining passion with those skills. Passion is what takes those skills to a whole new level. Being a doctor is easy; having the passion to truly want to help people is what really makes people better. A patient could drive 5 minutes and run into dozens of healthcare providers, but could they find one that is passionate about helping people reach their full potential? Or do the doctors only see the patient as a number, to help pay the bills?

When you develop passion for helping others, within your field of choice, you have already leveled up your potential for success. When you care for others, then ulterior motives don't have a chance. When we care about helping someone else to excel, then our minds race to find products, services, and ideas that will become an authentic passion for us to share with the world.

Triathlons became a passionate device for change in my life. It stayed that way for almost 20 years, because I never lost the feeling of the first triathlon I ever completed. It wasn't a very long race, but it was challenging, nonetheless. What I remember, and what I never lost, was the energy and the love and the fullness in my heart when I crossed the finish line. There was something about the challenge, the community, the inner battle, and the absolute unknown that charged my heart strings stronger than anything I had ever experienced before. I had found a sport that was bigger than sport alone. I had found a passion that, for the next 20 years, would charge everything I did with the same mentality of training. My passion for triathlons showed me that I was capable of doing anything and everything I put my mind to. Waking up early to get things accomplished became easy. Going the extra mile in training turned into going the extra mile at work, and with patients. Not quitting, 7 hours into a race, when it was all I wanted to do, turned into never letting myself quit in the real world — even when difficulty raised its ugly brow.

Lastly, the most important thing to do when you have found your passion is to express it as fast as you can. The journey of life is built on a commodity of time — the only commodity that we can't replenish, nor do we know how much is left in our tank. The "Make It Count" key for passion is not to die with the music still inside you. When your heart finds its music, don't hold back from sharing that music with the world. Open your mind and take action, immediately. Share the music with as many people as you can, because a passion-based idea is bound to have enormous impact on more people that you could ever imagine. The music contained in your heart may be the next great world-wide movement. It could be the next life-saving device, or it could be an app that brings us all closer together. Don't hold that potential game changer inside your heart, never to see the world. Speak up, stand tall, and spread your passion!

Make It Count Foundations

1. What has been weighing heavy on your heart lately that you want to do? What is stopping you from taking action?
2. List three things that you have done in your life that you are passionate about. What about these events created your passion?
3. Passion is an emotion that doesn't just show up. You need to invest some time within yourself, to uncover its potential. A quick activity, to uncover some potential passion in your life, is asking yourself what you would do if money wasn't an issue? What would you do, knowing that it would be a game changer, if you didn't have to worry about doing it for money upfront?
4. Passion is the driver behind most activities we do within our "Make It Count" days. Passion wakes us up, drives us to work harder, stops us from wasting precious time, pushes us harder at the gym, builds stronger relationships, stops us from eating unhealthy, makes us want to be there more for our kids, and passion is the fuel for all change.
5. We all know someone who lived a great life but didn't get to do exactly what they had planned. Whether they never started that new company, never told someone how much they loved them, or never found the courage to speak on stage — these people all kept the music inside them. Make a point today to take a moment and share your music with the world. People are waiting for the energy you possess, and they are thirsty for your passion.

Make It Counter: Binda Singh

Binda Singh was born and raised in rural Punjab, India, where his parents were farmers and his sisters learned to cook at a very young age. He and his two brothers worked on the farm and concentrated on their studies. In 1992, a teenage Binda came to Baltimore to join his brother Keir, who had come a few years earlier, and together they became some of the most acclaimed restaurateurs in Maryland. They had great success with their first venture, Banjara, in Federal Hill, and went on to have even longer-last success with the Ambassador Dining Room in the Tuscany/Canterbury neighborhood. His sisters later joined as chefs, making the restaurant a full family operation. After more than 20 years in the business, Binda opened the doors to Ananda, his crowning achievement in restaurants.

When he's not greeting customers and managing operations at Ananda, Binda enjoys spending time with his family, particularly his son Benjamin, who is his other most proud achievement!

You have an amazing capacity to make every single person you come in contact with feel like they are the most important person in the world. What drives you to not only succeed, but excel at the customer experience?

Customer service is the key to success in the hospitality industry. Without it, nothing else matters, and your business won't be successful. You can have the best food to offer, but if the customer experience isn't impressive, it doesn't make an impact. I always want my restaurant to be a place where people feel comfortable and welcome. It's part of the reason we never have a sign on any of our restaurants. It's important that people feel they are in a place that feels like home, or a friend's house. And that experience includes building a connection with us. If we are the host of the party, we need to make sure our guests are happy. Every night is like a party at Ananda.

Ananda is consistently rated as one of the top Indian food restaurants in the state of Maryland. What three habits do you consistently pursue that you think helps drive this consistency?

The three habits I've developed are:

1. Constantly striving to improve our menu. For many years at our previous restaurants, our menus stayed the same, year after year. At Ananda, it has become my passion to develop new dishes with my sister Kinday, who is our executive chef. I enjoy developing flavor combinations that capture people's attention and keep them interested. We have so many regular customers and we don't want them to get bored.

2. Pushing the quality control in the kitchen and on our restaurant floor at all times. I'm watching what's going on in the kitchen, and I see many of the dishes before they hit the dining room. From the way something is prepared, to the way it is plated, I want to personally ensure that I'm happy to put my name on every dish that goes out to a guest. On the restaurant floor, I'm making sure my staff are on-point, and the setting is perfect. Whether it's the temperature of the room, or the way the linens are laying on the table, everything matters.

3. Taking care of myself so I can perform at my best at all times. It's important that I look and feel my best whenever I'm representing my businesses. It's also a huge thing in my culture to be well groomed. Sikh men take pride in our appearance, and it brings us closer to God. In addition to presenting well from the outside, I need to take care of myself from within. I eat well, I meditate, and I work out as part of my regimen for being well.

What is your earliest memory of success and how does that memory help with your success today? What is your biggest failure that has led to your success?

The first time I truly felt successful was about a year after I came to the states. The day I arrived in Baltimore from my voyage from India, my brother Kehar had opened a new restaurant in Baltimore called Banjara. It was his place, but I worked there and learned the ropes. About a year later, Kehar took a trip to Italy for two weeks. I was left in charge of the restaurant, and I did surprisingly well. We actually had record high sales during those two weeks, so I felt like I had really done something right!

There was a time before that when I *thought* I was successful, but I had no idea what was really coming my way. I distinctly remember the first time that I started waiting tables after many months of washing dishes. I thought I had really made it!

Kehar and I had one huge failure that we were able to surpass and turn into a success. We had Banjara at the time, and we were looking to open a second restaurant. There was a restaurant in Towson, owned by a Greek man and we were interested in buying it. We negotiated a deal with the man, and we shook on it. He said he needed to go back to Greece to take care of his ailing mother. We wrote him a $10,000 check as a deposit for the purchase of his restaurant, based on our good-faith handshake. He took our check and ran off to Greece, never to return. Apparently, the bank was foreclosing on his restaurant. About a month later, The Ambassador Dining Room turned up, and it was the perfect place! It was a total game changer for us. We cut our losses with the Greek place and invested in starting up the high-end Indian restaurant at the Ambassador. Had we invested further in the Towson location, we would not have had the available capital to pick up the Ambassador. We dodged a bullet there!

What is one piece of advice that you would give to a younger version of yourself?

Take more chances and follow your gut. I was a bit timid about taking chances when I was younger, because I didn't have anything to fall back on. Now I know that taking chances is how you make big leaps forward, and it's the only way to really get what you want.

What do the words "Make It Count" mean to you?

Everything in life needs to matter. Anything that doesn't matter has no place in my life. I don't do anything part-way. Every interaction with a friend, customer, or family member must have meaning and be full of purpose. Every business venture needs to have my whole heart and soul in it.

If you only had two hours a day to devote to Ananda, what would you do with that time to move the needle?

If my time was limited that drastically, I would spend most of that time building a culture in the restaurant that emulates what I do on a daily basis. Everyone on the team would need to chip in on the responsibilities that I have put on my own shoulders. I've taken ownership of every task, but with a limited amount of time, I would have to delegate and ensure that everyone would do things exactly as I would do them, in order for me to feel comfortable with surrendering that control.

You and your brother are both very successful restaurateurs. What piece of advice would you give someone thinking of opening a restaurant that is more than just putting out good food?

Normally I tell people, "Don't do it!" I'm half-way joking, but at the same time I know that it's one of the most challenging careers to maintain. In all seriousness, I prefer to tell people that they need passion in their work, and they need to emulate what they are passionate about in their restaurant business.

What are your top three non-negotiables in life that help you lead a life of purpose?

Spending time with family, always feeling passionate about my career, and staying close to my roots.

CHAPTER 16

Monotasking

"Anything worth doing is worth doing well."

- Hunter S. Thompson

How many times in your life have you said that you were an incredible multitasker, and that you were proud of that title? How many times have you been asked in an interview if you were a good multitasker? What if I were to tell you that that's all made up, and that being a multitasker meant absolutely nothing?

There are those in the world who seem to be amazing at supertasking: whose accomplishments make it look like they are crushing multiple activities all at once, but in reality they are just very efficient with their time and actions. The word, "multitasking," originally started in the 1960's as it related to the efficiency of computers. Not long after, humans started to use it as a badge of honor for accomplishment. We have equated our success so much to being good multitaskers that I think we've really lost track of what's important. We've started to increase our activities to the point that we feel like we're busy accomplishing many things at once, but we really are busy doing things at a below average success rate.

In recent years, I have read many studies that have shown that interruptions as brief as just two seconds were enough to double the amount of errors a participant made in a mental task. Do we really ever focus on a single task anymore in 2018? We have a phone in hand, social media open, TV on in the background, music playing, dogs barking, and kids going in three different directions.

I fell into the multitasking trap for many years until I realized I wasn't executing anything the way I wanted or deserved to. I was crushing my "to do" list, but I felt that my results weren't anything stellar. I was successful, but none of it was at the standard that I expected from myself. I read an article on "monotasking" and, like most new things, scuffed at the idea of only focusing on one thing at a time. But since my results had been subpar, I thought, "Why not give it a shot?" And I went all in on monotasking.

After a few days, not only was I crushing my goals, but I found that I had never felt more accomplished in my life. The art of monotasking allowed me to singularly focus on a task, while minimizing potential interruptions until that task was either completed or well on its way to completion. It allowed me to fully invest myself in the moment, because it took my mind away from multiple cognitive distractors.

Sometimes when we try to do too much work, we end up doing nothing at all. We make such small progressions that it can be overwhelming when we are not making the progress that we ultimately desire. The difference between multitasking and monotasking comes down simple attention. Part of living in a "Make It Count" world is that we are focusing our attention span on only the most important pieces of our day. We are focusing on those simple segments that have the most bang for their buck so that we can fully enjoy everything that life has to offer. When we multitask, we are not attentive to any one thing because our mindset has gone adrift with differing priorities. Multitasking is just switching attention from one activity to another activity at a quick pace, and likely without the focus that the activity deserves. When we monotask, the attention is 100% geared toward that singular activity. We can fully squeeze all the juice out of that event, to make sure we are not only fully present but also getting the most out of that event, for ourselves and for our circle.

When we switch quickly from activity to activity, there is a much greater potential for burnout, fatigue, and frustration. One way to adjust and fight off the ill effects of multitasking is to map out what your perfect day will look like. While our days are never the same, and life always throws twists and turns into the mix, we can have a vision in our mind of what the ideal day looks like. This activity creates a vision of time management and determines what is important to us so we don't get sidetracked with activities that are inefficient.

From the time you'll wake up, to the time you'll exercise, to the time you'll write, eat, leave for work, read to your kids, do homework, meditate, go to bed — this activity will give you a framed outline of what you have time for in the day. There will always be items that pop up, and need to fit into your routine, but at least now you can decide which items are most beneficial to your time. The goal with this is to be efficient in making your day count. Don't be cluttered down by this idea so that your busy items are the low hanging fruit that don't have macro implications in your life. As you can see, the benefits for structure and monotasking can have larger, positive benefits.

The three benefits that have helped me the most are as follows:

1. **Rediscover yourself** — How often do you get so busy focusing on everything that you lose track of what is important? We create this multitasking "to do" list that wreaks havoc on our brain and not taking the time to do what's most important to us. My childhood dentist — who also occasionally filled the role of "dad," when I needed him to — was diagnosed with brain cancer just few years ago. Instead of packing it in and giving up, he fought as hard as he could to win. He sold his dental practice and made it his life's mission to "Make It Count." Instead of living in the crazy multitasking world, he and his wife began traveling as their personal mission in life. They committed to monotasking their most important thing, which was time with each other. They have since traveled near and far, but always do it together. They have rediscovered what is

important to them through balancing out the havoc that can invade our day to day structure.

2. **Increase creativity** - When we can step away from the chaos of a crazy lifestyle, or the distractions of multitasking, we can quiet the mind and boost creativity ten fold. As a lifelong runner, I used to love my training sessions. They would crush me, but in a way that always prepared me for the upcoming race. However, the sessions that I loved the most were the recovery runs, where it was just me and the world. My breathing was controlled, and I could mentally escape reality for some time with my thoughts. This was the time when I would schedule each week and bring my biggest creative obstacles with me on the run, because I knew by the end that I would have them solved with a new sense of energy and excitement. This monotasking allowed me to focus squarely on what I needed to accomplish, and my execution was typically precise and on point. When I got injured and couldn't run, I fell into a funk — not because I couldn't run, but because life took away my creative outlet. So, I jumped into this book without hesitation, because I knew it would provide me with the monotasking stage of focusing on what's important. The key is to fight back when life tries to make you too busy, or it takes away your outlet. Find something new that will allow you to focus on the present time and boost that creative genius.

3. **Be present** — Take a minute to put yourself into the original scenario from this chapter: TV on, phone in hand, social media up, music in the other room, doorbell ringing, spouse mowing the lawn, dinner on the stove, vacuuming the kitchen, kids asking for attention, and so on. All of these happen almost daily in my household, and all of them fight for my attention. The key is deciding whether you go all in, or if you divide and conquer. Monotasking allows you to divide and conquer, which allows you to be present in the moment. I could easily tell my kids to go play outside, but monotasking creates a list of what is most important to me at every second of my life. When I focus on them, I let my monkey mind know that other items can wait. Suddenly, I am present and fully enjoying my time with them without being distracted by items that won't matter the next day. When we focus, we can be present and fully engage in the journey to living out our legacy.

None of this is meant to be easy, especially when you have defined your excellence as being a multitasker in the past. Here is a challenge for you: next time you meet a friend for coffee, or your kid needs your attention, sit down and pay full attention to what is in front of you. Research has shown that even the simple multitasking of conversation, and occasionally sneaking a peak at your phone, decreases your emotional connection with the other person. Are you at full attention when you glance at your phone every few minutes? The simple goal of monotasking is to go in on one task at a time, to maximize its advantage in your life.

Make It Count Foundations

1. Multitasking creates distraction in actions, because we never get to be 100% fully involved in any one activity.

2. Find one creative outlet that allows you to focus on your thoughts. Running works well for some people, journaling is a great endeavor for others, but the key is to find an activity that inspires creativity without distraction.

3. Monotasking creates a new sense of adventure. We can get excited about just one thing at a time, with excellence.

4. Research has debunked the efficiency of multitasking. You are essentially just switching your attention from one activity to another.

5. Try writing down what your perfect day would be. This is a powerful exercise to learn what matters the most to you and it will give you a good outline of what needs to get done.

Make It Counter: Kary Brock

Kary Brock, a 2018 *Sports Business Journal* 40 Under 40 Award winner, brings marketing experience across agency, media, brand and property roles. Currently, Brock oversees the account team for Anheuser-Busch within the Endeavor Global Marketing Group. One of Brock's primary roles at Endeavor is managing the strategy for the entire US sports portfolio for AB - overseeing direction and activation across such properties as the NFL, NHL, MLB, NBA, golf, running, NASCAR, college sports, soccer, esports, surfing, UFC and other. Previously, she has overseen all marketing efforts for the IMG's College division leading a group responsible for ideating, developing, positioning and pitching successful sponsorship and brand strategies for new partners.

What is your earliest memory of success?

Winning the local Oratorical contest in New Jersey. This was a competition where one would write a five-minute speech on a specific topic and then present it. Even though I progressed throughout the competition, it was the first time I learned the connection of working hard, doing my best and it being noticed. I remember my mom making me practice over and over again in the kitchen as she made dinner. When the competition came, there was an expectation as to who the favorites were. Mentally, I already had placed myself behind those that we "knew were the winners." I remember thinking how nervous I was, how I wanted to do a good job, how I didn't want to forget any part of the speech or 'performance'. I had always been a rather quiet child and this was much more outgoing than I ever was in the past. So this not my typical personality and out of my comfort zone. But somehow, I didn't really think about it at the time and I made a conscious effort to try something. When I gave my speech, I remember not comparing myself to anyone when I was on stage and I just focused on what I wanted to do. It was one of the first memories of me just trying something. Regardless of the outcome push to experiment and prepare as best you can. I think I still have the note cards I practiced with and when I hear, "If Only," I still think of the speech.

You recently won the prestigious Forty Under 40 Award in the sports business world. That is a coveted honor within the sports industry that many aspire to, but never receive. What does the award mean to you, and what habits do you think you possess that have helped you along the way?

It was a honor to receive the Forty Under 40 Award and if I'm going to honest, I am still surprised it happened. Very early on in my career, I focused on the award after having completed a submission for my client at the time. I remember thinking how much he had accomplished and how he had influenced the sports industry. I looked at who had come before me and how much they had achieved. I hoped that I would participate in our industry in such a manner. I worked hard over the next several years, making sure I was pushing myself to represent my clients, company and my ideals the best way I could.

I am one of those people who focus on something and aggressively pursues that goal... whether it is first place at counties (my high school track meet), getting into a specific college, earning a promotion, or receiving an award. I learned and believe that hustle beats out a lot of things. While I may not be the brightest bulb on the tree, something I have realized is I will hustle to make sure I know what I need to know. While there is an element of the "fake it 'til you make it" approach, I have found it pushes a me to evaluate what I want and make efforts to achieve it. Throughout my career, every obstacle or hurdle has pushed me to foster my ability to adapt and evolve.

What is your greatest failure in life, and what did you learn from it?

This one is the hardest for me because I don't think I look at things as failures. Things may not go how I had hoped they would, but I try to learn from them while also adapting to the new course.

You have been an extremely successful executive for some of the top firms within the sports world, for many years. What piece of advice would you give someone coming out of college, wanting to eventually be in your shoes?

An incredible compliment to receive, and while I might tone down the "extremely successful" part, I certainly have been fortunate to have been afforded the opportunity to do some really cool things. Advice that I would give to a person starting in our industry is, at a minimum, threefold:

- Learn from everyone - up, down, sideways, diagonally: Everyone comes from different paths and you always, always have something to learn from anyone. And sometimes, what you learn from someone is actually what not to do.

- Ask for what you want: Something I learned is that you can't get something that you don't ask for, i.e., higher salary, advanced title or a larger role. The worst that can be said is "no," but you at least have put it out there for people to think about.
- This. Is. Business.: I realize this may sound a little more aggressive than intended and I am not saying to be cutthroat or unethical. Rather, go into a conversation with the facts and a point of view. Facts cannot be argued and while they might be met with opinions, facts are facts. If you've developed your POV, certainly listen to opinions because they might make your POV stronger, or they might not.

You have worked with numerous professional athletes at the top of their game. Is there a common personality trait that you have noticed that sets some of them apart?

Attitude and outlook. You face high highs, low lows and medium mediums. Throughout all of it, you have to stay grounded in your outlook and attitude. Remind yourself of the why and stay the course. Try not to be affected by those external factors.

If you could put a saying on a billboard, what would it say and why?

Can I have two billboards? One would say, "*Throw glitter in today's face*" and the other, "*Be Present*". The second is so important in today's world of no one actually experiencing the world fully and in real time due to social media, posting, etc.

What person or event has had the biggest impact on your life?

This was an easy one. County championships my senior year in high school. My season long rival and I had run the same time leading into the 400 Individual Hurdles Finals. My dad had prepped me going into the race that I needed to amend my typical approach and go out hard in the first half of the race. Typically, I hung back for the first half of the race and chased down the field over the last 200 meters. As the race started, I applied my dad's coaching and focused on my race vs. the field. I focused on my steps and the hurdles that were in front of me. There were actually three of us neck and neck at the eighth (of 10) hurdle. At the ninth hurdle, one of the girl's steps were off and she fell off the lead. I ran stride for stride with my rival as we approached the 10th hurdle. I felt confident in my steps and form, albeit tired. I took the last hurdle with the other girl misstepping and falling behind. I won. All of this was to teach me to run my own race. Don't compare yourself. Don't chase someone else. Focus on what you want and what you know how to do.

What do you think it means to live a "Make It Count" lifestyle?

Purpose. Be purposeful in everything you do. In what you say and how you say it. In what you do and how you do it. In how you interact with people and how you interact with yourself (the last being the most important).

"Make It Count" extra thoughts;

I think something to consider is something I just read about the "Right Recording". Essentially, it's about having the right soundtrack playing in your head for your life and what you do. I'm not sure if this is applicable for where your book is going, but I think there is something to it. The basic idea here is that you need to be kind to yourself. With everything coming at us on a daily basis, it's important to make sure our mind is sound. We need to make sure our brain is taking in the right messages and throwing away those that may not be accurate, helpful, productive or healthy. More so, the folks who succeed (or those we believe have success from our vantage point) have the same challenges with mental soundtracks that we do. I know I have a challenge with it constantly.
I leave you with this because I think it sums up the theory perfectly (and me, frankly) - - "Sometimes I amaze myself and sometimes I put the laundry in the oven."

CHAPTER 17

Manage Emotions

"An eye for an eye makes the whole world blind."

- Mahatma Gandhi

Feeling emotions is what makes life so rich and full. The ability to create emotions of love, passion, confidence, and happiness is what all of us strive for. And for the most part, we hit it out of the ballpark. It's when we lose focus and let our paradigms shift that the emotions of fear, doubt, disappointment, and anger creep in, and we need someone to help us in managing our emotions.

Negative emotions are destructive by nature — they make us focus too much on the past, worry about the future, lose sight of our gifts, and even treat those around us in unfortunate ways. Emotions are a choice that we need to manage, but the ability to manage them only comes with practice. It comes with being able to identify your emotions, and to recognize that they need to change. Emotions are tricky, in the sense that when we are in a bad mood or something has set us off, we respond based on that emotion and not on what's productive. We get cut off in traffic and the first thing we want to do is honk, give them the number one sign, or express some explicit language that we then have to apologize to our kids for. That emotion comes out in pure response, and sometimes it becomes a permanent response depending on what happens next. Anger in traffic could lead to an accident, or even worse. Just like everything else in life, it's important to always take a second before responding. Evaluate where the emotions are in that moment, and make the choice then based on what is necessary.

Most reactions that lead us down the wrong path are based on unnecessary emotions. Just as Gandhi said in the quote that began this chapter: if we go about life looking for revenge, then we will never experience long term success. I hear it all the time from my children. When I ask them why they did something they shouldn't have, they always say, "I did it because she made me angry" or "I did it because she hit me." Each of these reactions are based on emotions in the moment that caused them to behave in a way that didn't move the needle forward like actions should. As I stated before, feeling emotions makes life rich. We just need to have the strategies in place to manage those emotions, so that they are not taking us to a place that becomes permanent.

Steps to Manage Emotions:

1.   **Awareness** — We have roughly 70,000 thoughts running through our heads each and every day. I am sure that some individuals who have not learned to manage emotions probably jump up over the 100,000 mark. With all of those thoughts, there is the likelihood that no matter how hard we try, a negative emotion will invade and take up residence for a little while in our mind. We know that this is okay it shows that we are human — the crisscrossing of

emotions in life makes us who we are. What is not okay is not being aware of these emotions and how we need to process them. The awareness that you are losing your cool, as they say, is crucial to managing your emotions. If you are not aware in the first place, then how can you possibly take any next step? One key strategy in the "Make It Count" mentality is to pay very close attention to the body. Have you ever noticed, when your emotions turn negative, that your posture changes? Your shoulders hunch forward, your head tilts down, and you don't have posture of a confident individual. Some people also start to sweat, as the sympathetic nervous system starts to take effect. You go into your flight and fight mode, and now your body says it's time to get angry and battle. Look in the mirror for a reminder of your physical posture if your awareness is starting to blink red. Have you ever seen a negative emotion that produced a smile? No, usually the reflection the mirror is working hard to produce is a face of disgust, anger or "Why me!?" So, the first step is to become aware that you are in the process of a negative emotion.

2. **Take a step back** — Just like in the chapter on becoming a better listener where we think before we speak in order to make sound, intelligent responses. Managing emotions involves the same brief break in doing one thing before you do something else. When you become aware of your negative state is the time to briefly halt your progress to understand what your next move is. The key is not to make a move that will result in a permanent action you will regret. If someone comes at you with a negative opinion, it's best to think before you respond. If your boss tells you that your work stinks, take a second to analyze where they are coming from which will help you understand your response. People will naturally try and stir up some type of negative emotion throughout your day. My question to you is do you want to step down to their level or rise up and hopefully bring their way of thinking out of the gutter and to a productive Make It Count state?

3. **Bigger picture** — The bigger picture of life always revolves around the simple concept of time. We really don't know how much time we have on the life clock. We could have days or we could have years. Why waste time over negative emotions when there is so much good that still needs to be done? Why stress over the bad grade, that you didn't make the team, that someone said you looked goofy or that you didn't get the job. All these are temporary actions or opinions that should be more fuel for your fire then something that sidetracks you from progress. Most things that we stress over, get angry from or develop a fear of

have no real bearing in your future. I understand some people have phobias that are strong or lose a job that really impacts their family but even those two options, with the right approach, are temporary. Big picture is our true lack of time in this journey so don't waste that precious time over things that don't matter.

4. **Develop an outlet** — The outlets for emotional management are enormous and comes down to what you enjoy. If you hate writing because it is boring, then journaling or writing out your thoughts might not be the best outlet for your emotions. My wife knows that exercise is my outlet. My events impact my emotions and they feel like they are compounding faster than I can control my wife is typically the first person to say, "go workout and you will feel better." Guess what? She is always right! Exercise provides me the option to focus, accomplish and return back to my routine with a calm, collected mind and understanding of what my task at hand is. So next time you're feeling stressed, upset, sad or depressed, go for a hike, a run, write out your monkey mind on paper, have coffee with a friend, play video games, read a book, paint a picture, listen to your favorite band, play an instrument, watch your favorite show or practice the fine art of meditation. Just make sure that you have an outlet that brings your mind back to a positive state of forward progress.

5. **Make managing emotions a habit** — The first four steps are null and void and a waste of time if they don't become habit in your life. Sure, for a couple of days you can be aware when your mindset is changing. Sure, for a couple of days you can realize that life is a precious commodity. Sure, for a couple of days you can go for a run when you can't control your emotions. However, if these just last a couple days and you are right back into the mix of letting your negative emotions run your life then the steps didn't have enough impact in your life. The truth is this will happen. Even the most successful people on this planet falter from time to time. What makes them successful is they are uber aware of the importance of their habits. When they have a hiccup in their routine, it doesn't take them long to bring the habit back or course correct the habit and make it stronger.

Do you know why emotions are so strong and such an integral part of our lives, regardless of whether they are negative or positive? It's because of the limbic system, which is the oldest part of your brain and the central hub for dealing with emotions. The limbic system developed first, and it has been the most active part of our human brains for a long time. This active system allows us to process and feel life. One thing not to do with the limbic system is to try and suppress its action. Trying to suppress bad emotions is like dusting the dirt under the rug in hopes that it will disappear. Negative emotions will not just disappear if we try to suppress them. They will always be there, no matter how hard we try to get rid of them.

The key, as mentioned before, is to know they are present and to have an action plan for making them beneficial. Some people stress over the possibility of change. The worry, stress and fear of change occupies more space in the mind than it should. Change, at the end of the day, is a good thing. When we visualize and accept change as a positive event, then we allow ourselves to feel what the next step should be. Ignore change, and it allows the negative emotions to build.

The idea of "Make It Count" is to attack each day like it's the best day we have ever had, because we are not sure when it will be our last day. When negative emotions infiltrate this process, it's hard for us to be completely engaged in what we need to do to accomplish great things. My wife and I agreed many years ago that one strategy that we would engage in was to never go to bed angry. This has allowed us to talk things out, that before we might have pushed off to the next day. But, most importantly, it has allowed us to wake up the next day, ready to crush the day together. We don't bring the baggage from the previous day over into the current day. We get to start from where we left off the night before, and from there we can keep attacking what needs to be done along our journey. Carrying baggage from the past just slows down our process. It impedes our ability to "Make It Count!"

Make It Count Foundations

1. Emotions are not a bad thing because they are what makes life rich. We need passion to go forward in life.

2. The key to identifying emotions is choosing not to respond in a way that could be permanent. Thinking before you react means you won't regret doing something you shouldn't have, simply because an emotion clouded your judgement.

3. When you get stressed, angry, fearful, or doubt yourself, what do you do? Have you been able to identify the outlets in your life that engage in the optimistic, growth mindset? What are three things that you love to do? How could you input these activities into your life to help manage emotions?

4. We shouldn't avoid emotions, but, instead, take time to plan out situations that limit our exposure to certain negative situations that may cause unwanted emotions. If you know that traffic is going to make you upset, then leave a little earlier to avoid the stress. If you know that a certain coworker's opinions always seem to ruffle your feathers, then either go out of your way to be kind to them or let them do their thing while you move on with the bigger picture.

5. Try the concept of never going to bed angry. Leave your emotions within the bookends of each day. Don't let today's negativity have an impact on tomorrow's positivity.

Make It Counter: Britt Oergel

Britt Oergel is a Sales Leader who has worked in the cancer diagnostics arena for the past 15 years. She has grown her career working as a rep and then strategic accounts, then manager then V.P. At each level she really tries hard to absorb all the things that she needs to know to continue her climb. Britt has reached a level where she can balance the most important success in her life: her family (3 daughters and driven, successful husband). Professionally, she is fulfilled and doesn't need to keep climbing the ladder. She would rather make her role super strong and balance her work and life.

What is your favorite quote and why?

"Be the change you wish to see in the world" - Mahatma Gandhi. This speaks to the idea that in order for anything to be different you have to change the approach. You can live a life of status quo but then you know what you get. If you really want to see something change its trajectory, then you have to do something different.

Professionally, you reached an executive level status early in your career. What is the biggest thing you have learned from becoming an executive at a young age?

Don't put off tomorrow what you can do today. This is easier said than done. I think that many times we tend to work on what is easy rather than pushing ourselves to really challenge what we can accomplish all day every day. We get caught up in doing the minimal amount of work to get by rather than driving all we can to drive our successes. I have always been a wildly accountable person. Did I do enough? Can I do more? What can I do differently to get a better outcome? How can I ensure a better result next time? I think this bodes well in my professional development and has helped me break through glass ceilings. Also, I have surrounded myself with people that always expect more and better! I have reps I work with who constantly show me better ways to do the same thing and managers who invest on my success.

What piece of advice would you give a younger version of yourself?

Allow failures as it molds who you become. I think that in the younger years I would almost be negatively affected by my non-success (even in sports): if I failed I didn't do something right. Now I take that as an opportunity to grow and tweak my to go forward plan. This helps me keep getting better and better at what I do. This applies in my personal life as much as my professional life. I am going through each step as a wife and parent on new roads I am paving. I don't always do things right but when I am not happy with the direction, I course correct.

If you only had two hours a day to perfect your craft, what would you do?

I would write a list of the most important things I need to get done in that two hours and knock off the most impactful ones first. This way I stay focused on what needs to be done and challenge myself to get to as many of my items as possible.

You have had the privilege of managing people at a very young age. What do you think are two crucial qualities of a successful leader that others could incorporate into their paradigms?

I think there are many more than 2 qualities that you must have. You have to allow people to do for themselves, and not do for them. This was a tough lesson as a new manager because I thought that it was "my way or the highway" and it's amazing that there are so many ways to accomplish the same tasks. Continue to provide personal development in each of your people that you manage so that they feel fulfilled. You are only as good as your team. If they feel determined and driven to be successful due to ways that you provide development then everyone wins

What is your definition of success?

Success is allowing yourself to fail and learn from your mistakes. To approach your business in different ways. Laying the groundwork and reaching a summit so that you see the fruits of your labor pay off. Being able to revel in little wins so that you don't always feel defeat if you aren't hitting your strides and smiling through it all because whatever you are doing is making an impact.

What is your definition of "Make It Count?" How do you apply the "Make It Count" mantra to your daily log?

I think "Make it Count" means that we cannot take life for granted. Tomorrow is not guaranteed so it's super important to absorb all the great things life has to offer. I am super blessed to have a supportive, loving partner and 3 wonderful children who keep reinventing my focus. My life is forever changed with my family in it. I have always struggled with the work/life balance but I know that my family helps me keep front and center how to make life count. Work is what I do to provide for my family but I am super passionate to work in a field that helps people. That makes my days in my professional world count. Since I am lucky to be the wife of the author, we have lived the motto "Make it Count" officially for the last 6-7 years. I think it has really helped our family dynamic to know that you have to make every second count. We don't waste moments because they are too precious

Life is about balance and once that balance is off, it's hard to "Make It Count." How do you balance being an incredible mom, an amazing entrepreneurial business woman, a friend to all, and one who never turns down a challenge?

I think that it's something called boundaries. I didn't have them in the past and work won. It's not important in my life to keep driving my focus or business if I can't balance it with the people who mean the most to me. I try really hard to be present when I am home and during crazy, sports filled weekends so that my family and friends know how important they are to me. I also want my team to know when I am with them, they have my undivided attention. There is a motto I have started living by that really is defined by Make it Count- I have to work to live not live to work! I constantly try to ensure that my family knows how important they are to me while balancing a professional career that is very demanding.

CHAPTER 18

Better Questions – Better Answers

"Quality questions create a quality life. Successful people ask better questions, and as a result, they get better answers."

- Tony Robbins

As a kid, I was curious about everything. Growing up in a age when the only news source was a newspaper or the local news (which we never watched), I always had so many questions. I was definitely that kid who wore out the word "why." My mom humored me for probably way too long, and then one day she challenged me by telling me that *better questions get better answers*. She insisted that if I really wanted to learn, I had to first learn how to ask the right questions. Everyday she taught me that *questions have the power to create change*. And later, I used this same philosophy with my kids as they started to grow cognitively. I preached the same things my mom did, and I insisted that the power was within them to not only ask better questions, but also to learn how to get deeper into the answers they were looking for.

Questions fulfill the need we all have to connect on a deep and honest level. They allow us to help others who are going through hardship and allow us to get to a new daily meaning of the purpose of our journey. When used in the right manner, they can empower people.

Take a great leader, for example. This person doesn't stand in front of a group, and just speak for the sake of speaking. They engage with their audience. Their questions don't seek "yes or no" responses, but they require the listener to take a second and think deeply how they would like to respond. An incredible leader offers questions geared toward changing the landscape of business, community, people, and the world for the better. Great communicators teach people to communicate in a way that awakens human potential, empowers actions, respect, and brings out the best in those around us. Great questions have the ability to disarm people. If, as a leader, I asked one of my employees, "Why did you do this?" I would get a response that was based in the wrong emotions. The person could potentially close off any and all learning capacity from this point forward, because they are answering as a form of defense. Instead, the more beneficial question might be, "What did you learn from this, and how can we make it better in the future?" The second question takes the blame away from that one person, and now it becomes more of a team effort toward what can be done differently in the future.

Also, that second question opens up the potential for the employee to have some ownership in decisions — both personal and for the company. A great starting point for questions is in the questions we ask ourselves. It's hard to ask great questions, when we are not being 100% authentic with ourselves from the start. We can't ask deep questions or learn how to get great answers, if we don't answer our own questions appropriately.

Do these questions and answers sound familiar?

Why didn't I get the promotion? The boss just doesn't appreciate me.
Why aren't I losing weight? I am following the plan.
Why are my 5K times not getting faster? I am just not a gifted runner.
How am I supposed to wake up early to start a morning routine when I am so tired? Mornings aren't my thing.

Now, let's reframe these questions to be more specific...

What am I not doing that could be the reason for not getting the promotion? I have been showing up late to meetings consistently which shows I am not as committed as I should be.
Have I been following the weight loss plan 100% according to plan? I follow it Monday through Thursday, but on the weekends I really like to unleash and eat or drink whatever I want.
Am I doing all I can to become faster runner? I have not been following my nutrition plan, I have completely ignored my nutrition plan and I am doing the same workout over and over which makes me feel stale mentally.
What can I change in my life to try and become a morning person? I can stop watching TV at nighttime, eat a sensible dinner at a reasonable time and develop habits to encourage a morning routine worth living for.

Make it a routine to always work on asking yourself better questions, and also realize that there is no such thing as a *wrong* question. The great interviewers of history, like Larry King, say that sometimes asking a simpler question is the key to asking a better question. Mr. King goes into detail on simple questions to produce better answers in an interview for the Jesse Thorn podcast, *The Turnaround.* All too often, interviewers try to get too detailed too fast and their initial question is often longer than the answer itself. It's better to keep questions simple because we are using them to build dialogue. Simple questions also avoid the problem of asking multiple questions at once. If I was to ask you, "Who has been the most influential person in your life? What did they teach you? What principles do you take away from their influence? How has it changed you? And have you taken that influence to help someone else?" All of these are sound questions, but they are likely to be distracting. Take a breath, take one step at a time, keep it simple, and focus on one question at a time.

Benefits of asking good questions:

1. **Show true care and compassion** — When we ask better questions, we are showing the person we are communicating with that we care about them. When we ask better questions, we are showing the other person our commitment to their improvement. Better questions not only get better answers, but they show the other person that we are listening. Listening feeds our recognition system with info to build our dialogue as we proceed. If we ignore feedback, and physical responses, and only questions to feed our own agenda, then the ability to connect with other people will be short lived. People open up when they are cared for and caring allows us the ability to build life-long rapport with our circle and community.

2. **Be open to learning** — Questions allow us to be selfish at times but in a good-natured way. We get to ask questions to get better answers which in turn allow us to learn unlimited amounts of information. If you don't like the answers you got, then ask better questions. If the answer doesn't make sense, then ask a better question to understand why. When we understand the why we grow exponentially over time in both a macro and micro environment.

3. **Improvement** — When we commit to asking better questions, we are committing to becoming a better version of yourself. We are seeking to become better communicators, we are seeking to become better mentors, we are seeking to become better parents, we are seeking to become better friends and simply seeking to become better humans.

4. **Go deeper** — You can learn so much about someone just by listening, but you have to know how to ask the questions that matter first. Depth of relationships are usually a result of the communicating factors that promote them. I know I can ask my wife superficially how her day was, or I can be present, look her in the eyes and ask, "Honey what made today special?" Deeper questions afford us deeper relationships in life and when our relationships grow, we become powerful simply through our affiliations with people we care for.

5. **Open ended questions allow for fulfillment** - This is something I had to learn fast as 50% of my job as a doctor is asking questions. I can tell you exactly what is wrong with you in my career now without ever really touching you. I have learned which questions draw the best answers out of patients. I have learned that open ended questions engage the other party to open up their response to more than a yes, no or maybe answer. We can get the most out of everything

we encounter when we really focus on open ended questions that bring out the most in every interaction.

In the end, your ability to communicate will help you develop a magnificent talent for making the most out of your day. When you "Make It Count," it's not just about improving your life, but about improving the life of those around you too. When you become proficient in asking the right questions, people will seek you out because they respect you. They will see you as someone who might know the answer, and as someone who makes them feel better after each and every interaction. Great questions improve people — plain and simple. That improvement is measured by the increased ability to make a difference in their life. If I focus on better questions, I help serve my daughter. If her life is improved through positive interaction, then she learns the importance of making others better. Then this continues to grow, all because I took the time to "Make It Count" via asking better questions.

Make It Count

Make It Count Foundations

1. Questions allow us to communicate with others in a way that awakens human potential, respect of others, empowerment, and quests to learn.

2. Great questions disarm other people, which opens the world up to more efficient communication.

3. Before you start pointing fingers, start by asking *yourself* the hard questions. If you can't answer your own questions on growth, then how are you capable of helping others?

4. There is no such thing as a wrong question, only a question that has not been reworked over time — to be as caring, compassionate, and powerful as it can be.

5. Work on asking open ended questions. When you ask questions that require a yes, no or maybe, you are not investing in the growth of the parties involved.

181

Make It Counter: Ron Tribendis

Ron Tribendis DC (Doctor of Chiropractic) is co-founder of Performance Medicine & Sports Therapy, a multidisciplinary facility impacting lives through innovative techniques, superior service, and applying a whole-body approach that sets the standard for sports medicine and recovery. He is a 20+ time Ironman Finisher and the host of *Recover with Purpose Podcast*.

You have built one of the top sports medicine and recovery brands in the world. Professional athletes travel far and wide just to get top notch treatment from Performance Medicine and Sports Therapy. What is the biggest lesson you have learned by building a successful brand?

Building a brand is something I always wanted to do. Mainly because I felt like I could help more people, without letting my ego get in the way. It was a way for me to not be so self-serving. With a brand I am able to include more people into the project; helping more people from a health care perspective and from a business perspective. I knew having "my name" on a building was very limiting and self serving. Building a brand helps create change. So, my number one lesson or advice...don't go it alone. Find your team. You will be more impactful in any profession choosing this route.

You have been very successful throughout your career, both professionally and in your personal space. Everything you do seems to turn to gold. What are your top 5 non-negotiables that allow you to be successful so consistently?

These are going to be very repetitive and things you have heard from other lifestyle and mindset coaches, but they work. 1. Exercise...healthy body = more endurance for your day. 2. Get up early and exercise. This is my win for the day, even if it is as simple as stretching. Running a business and having a family is demanding. Chances are if you put it off, it won't get done. 3. Nutrition. Over the past few years I have really dialed this in. I am far more productive with proper hydration, limited sugar, no bread or alcohol. 4. Read something every day. This keeps me creative. 5. Routine...everything I listed above requires you to find a routine.. motivation for a routine is a feeling...feelings aren't real... this takes discipline...discipline will get you out of bed in the morning, not motivation.

What is your favorite quote and why?

"You found your name, so grind it's a matter of time" – Rowlan. This is from a hip hop song called Born Hustler. I have to say this resonates with me the most at this point in my life. I put this song on when I need a reminder of what it takes...as far as I am concerned, we have built a brand, now we are grinding to make a difference in the sports medicine field. It's just a matter of time...nothing great EVER happened overnight. I need that reminder because I can be very impatient.

One of the chapters in this book is called "Listen More Than You Speak." You have developed a highly sought after podcast, called *Recover With Purpose*. How did you develop the skills needed to be such an incredible interviewer?

I decided to do the podcast for two reasons. One, it took me out of my comfort zone. I wanted to be a better speaker. What better way than to record yourself on a mic? I wanted to make sure I wasn't just talking to hear my own voice. I wanted to give back. I can only help 30 people a day in the office. With this medium I can try to help 100's or 1000's. Two, I talk with so many interesting people each day. I was being selfish; I wanted to talk to some longer. And if I was getting a benefit from what they were sharing, I believed more would benefit also.

What piece of advice would you give a younger version of yourself?

Be patient. Enjoy the process. I have a tendency to grind so hard that I don't take the time to enjoy the process.

What does your perfect day look like?

Wake early, coffee, read, workout, coffee, office, kid stuff, bed early...coffee might find its way in there in the afternoon. Lol

How has being an accomplished Ironman Triathlete helped the rest of your life?

Triathlons helped me develop routine, consistency, and a work ethic. They were qualities always there but triathlons helped me refine them. It's a sport that takes a long time to get good. Now that I am retired from the sport, I have carried over those principles to life and business.

What do the words "Make It Count" mean to you?

You only get one life. Live your best life and make it count.

CHAPTER 19

Fail With A Smile

"I have missed more than 9,000 shots in my career. I have lost almost 300 games. 26 times, I have been trusted to take the game winning shot and missed. I've failed over and over again in my life. And that is why I succeed."

- Michael Jordan

The *Merriam-Webster* definition of failure is: "a lack of success." It's a word that rings fear into the hearts of a lot of people. So, I ask you to reach into your pocket and come up with a definition for what *success* means to you. If failure is a lack of success, then I think it's important to first come up with a personal definition for success before we give "failure" any attention. As you'll find out in this chapter, both success and failure are just words to describe an action or an emotion. At the end of the day, everything within these words is up to us to decide — both what it means to us and how we will act and portray it in our daily lives.

As a society, we love to hear success stories and we get scared of stories of failure. We hide the stories of failure from the world in hopes that no one will find out. Why is that? Those success stories wouldn't be possible without dealing with failure along the way. If you ignored every turn that ended in failure, then the turn that ended in success would be off the grid. The goal in life *should,* instead, be to embrace failure for what it is.

The "Make It Count" definition of failure is "a learning process for success." No failure is permanent, as long as we acknowledge what is going on and take ownership of our next move. We assume failure is final, and are scared of it happening. Think of the failures we often hear: losing a job and feeling like a failure, a business fails, a sports team fails to advance, someone fails to lose weight during a fitness challenge, someone fails to wake up early, someone fails to get to work on time, someone fails to make it to their kid's performance, someone fails to write in their journal, fails to stay sober, fails to thank a neighbor for their gesture, fails to have the courage to get up on stage, fails a college final, or fails to make the varsity team at school. What do all these failures have in common? None of them are permanent. The key is taking ownership for the next action. The key is to avoid placing blame on anyone else and to resist avoiding the consequences of failure. When we do, the failure typically snowballs out of control.

Each of the failures above can be flipped on their edge, and when we own the failure the next step looks like this: a job was lost, so we can pursue a new passion; a business didn't work out, so now we can focus on what will work in the future; a sports team lost, so now the athletes can train harder for the next season; we failed to lose weight, so now we can be honest with our efforts and stop the cheat meals; we didn't wake up in time, so we know to set the alarm earlier; we were late to work, so now we can stay later to get more work done; we didn't pass the college final, so we hold ourselves accountable to study more; we didn't make the varsity team, so we change our mindset to accomplish our goal the next year.

The simplest action we can take, in order to make failure work for us, is to take ownership of the results. Ownership keeps the control in our court, and it allows us to learn from our actions. Ownership allows us to be in control of what happens next. The other simple step is to just smile. Since failure is crowded with so much fear, anxiety, and negative emotions, why not do the easiest thing to crush that dead-end action? Smile, smile, smile. The benefits of smiling have been researched to exhaustion and the results never change.

Benefits of smiling:

1. **Contagious** – Who are you drawn to at a party? It's always the person having a good time, smiling, and creating a positive environment.
2. **Foundation of youth** - Smiling creates a better outlook on life which improves all health metrics, motivates us to exercise, and keeps us focused on the goal instead of the distractions.
3. **Improve mood** - Watch any kid who is in a funk or bad mood. The second they smile, their nature and demeanor changes immediately. Smiling and laughter creates an environment of movement.
4. **Focus** - Smiling allows our mind to focus on the task at hand instead of being distracted by the actions that don't push us forward.
5. **Improved immune function** - Smiling decreases all of the hormones associated with bringing our immune systems down. Think of all the times you have been sick, and most are associated with sadness, stress and an environment of negativity.
6. **Lowers stress and anxiety** - Smiling decreases the stress hormone cortisol. Smiling improves your mood and allows you to focus on positive change.
7. **Releases endorphins -** As a lifelong runner always on a quest for the endorphin release, I can tell you that smiling and laughter increases endorphin release which allows us to feel like we can conquer anything.
8. **Better relationships** - Relationships that are built around stress and anxiety struggle to keep a strong foundation. Smiling, caring and compassionate environments form a strong bond within relationships which allow them to prosper and grow.
9. **Strong leadership** - Which leader sounds like someone you would rather work for? The leader who threatens and is always in a bad mood or the leader who promotes a creative environment and is always smiling?

So why fail with a smile? I think Winston Churchill said it best, "Success is the ability to go from failure to failure without losing your enthusiasm." If we fail and then pout, we create a "poor me" environment and we are choosing to let our dreams die with that one single failure. However, if we attack a failure with a smile, then our next steps are based in confidence, growth, education, leadership, and improvement. Thus, our dreams don't die but instead multiply by 10. People who live and die by their excuses constantly use failures as a crutch. They use that crutch to help them avoid any and all future failures. They use that crutch to essentially beat away any chance of future growth. Whether it's Steven Spielberg initially failing to get into USC film school, inventors failing thousands of times to produce a successful product, Steve Jobs getting fired from Apple, numerous successful authors having initial publishers slam the doors in their faces, or Michael Jordan getting cut from his high school team — the success stories are all built on each of these people learning from their failure, having a positive attitude, and getting to work on what the next step will be. The individual who is smiling and in a good mood is seldom looked at as a failure. They see everything as a growing opportunity. Their energy is undeniably strong and contagious, and others become thirsty to have what they have. It takes research and patience to uncover layers of failed decisions and actions that — while seeming catastrophic on paper — can be used as a lesson to fuel positive change. The benefits of failure could take up pages, but the top ten for most successful entrepreneurs and leaders are:

1. **Reality Check** - Every road, path and journey will be littered with hurdles, bumps and bruises. When we can accept that this event will happen then we can be ready and willing to accept and move on.

2. **Lessons** - Failure is the greatest educator. It teaches us what doesn't work or doesn't work in this moment. The key is to learn from it and figure out how to improve.

3. **Opportunities** - Failure creates opportunities as long as your eyes are open. You may fail at a business only to realize that in the failure you identified another business opportunity. Failure also gives us an opportunity to teach others a better way.

4. **Strength** - Failure only makes us stronger when we realize that failure is not long-term. We learn how resilient we can be that when we are cut, the scar comes back stronger.

5. **Accountability** - Ownership is the first step to take after a failure. Being accountable for your actions and deciding you want to be a leader of change allows the failure to be a success.

6. **Driver** – Failure, when you accept and understand failure, it can become a driver in our lives. It's not that we seek out failure, but we have to understand it is not as negative as we think. With the right path, that knowledge can take us up over the mountain.

7. **Fear** - Fear is a strong emotion but that's all it is: an emotion. Most things we fear never happen, but we give them so much energy. When we experience failure and realize, with the right principles, that we can be successful then we squash fears head on.

8. **Sharing** - Community can be your strongest driver to success. When you fail, call up your buddies for a coffee or lunch and share with them what happened. Use it as a teaching moment to help your community because when we teach, we reinforce positive behaviors in our foundational structure.

9. **Forge Ahead** - Like Winston Churchill said, go from failure to failure without losing your enthusiasm. Keep pressing forward not allowing anything to set you back. As with all "Make It Count" principles, the moment is now and memories come from these moments.

10. **Acceptance** - Accept that failure will happen and you have already won. Ignore them or run from them and you risk letting the failure become that snowball which never stops rolling until it's out of control.

It's time we restructured how we view words and the meaning we put behind their definitions. Think about how you interact with your circle during the day. Use failures as a teaching moment. When one of my kids fails, I tend to congratulate them more than telling them they did something wrong, but only when we discuss what they learned from the event. If they take nothing away from their failure, then they are destined to repeat it over and over again. However, when they acknowledge the failure and use it as a growth structure, then the positivity that flows from it is almost always beneficial. They learn what they did wrong, and then they are equipped to crush whatever they do next!

Redefine your metrics, develop a new foundation of what success and failure mean to you, learn to grow from every situation, and make every failure count.

Make It Count Foundations

1.   What has been your definition of failure up until this point in your life? That definition is how you view all struggles and growth.

2.   Look back on some of your biggest failures? What was the first response you had to the them?

3.   Smiling has the ability to not only reshape your current physiology but also the physiology of those around you. Next time you go to your favorite coffee shop, try this technique: greet the employee with a big smile, ask how their day is going and go out of your way to bring a positive atmosphere. I can guarantee that you will get positive energy in return, or at least help to turn around that individual's current mood.

4.   Some of the greatest success stories in history are only viewed by the money made or the fame acquired. However, if you ask the people behind the success stories what they learned during their journey, you are more than likely to get stories back of struggle, failure and the hard times. These hard times help define how hard we work and how much passion we need to bring to each situation.

5.   Failure's most powerful tool is as an educational piece. When investments go wrong, we fail a test, we don't make an athletic team or miss out on a promotion, there is typically a piece of information to be learned from each event. What could you have done more? What type of routines could you have added? What type of relationships could you have networked and what did you do wrong that you now see with the benefit of hindsight? Learning is a tool we must never quit on. Moments, memories and adventures are full of movements for us to become better and adjust to "Make It Count!"

Make It Counter: Charlotte Canning

Charlotte Canning is the Vice President of Brand and Culture and third generation owner of Hoffer Plastics Corporation. Shas 20 years of experience in Sales and Marketing.

Charlotte graduated from Purdue University with a BS in Business Management and went on to start her career working for Northwestern Mutual in their Sales department. In 2001, Charlotte relocated to New York City and started a career with Pepsi Lipton Partnership (a joint venture between Pepsico and Unilever) covering the Northeast region for foodservice. She eventually moved back to Chicago and assumed responsibility for the Midwest region.

In 2006, Charlotte joined the Hoffer family business as a Business Development Manager. In 2012, she was promoted to Director of Marketing and worked to create and lead the company's internal marketing efforts. In 2015, Charlotte was promoted to Vice President of Brand and Culture and took responsibility for leading the Human Resource team while continuing to focus on marketing.

Charlotte has been married for 16 years to her husband, James, and has 2 beautiful daughters, Colbie (9) and Cora (5). Outside of work, she spends her free time volunteering for local non-for-profits and sits as a board member for both United Way of Elgin and Cal's Angels

What piece of advice would you give a younger version of yourself?

Two things come to mind. 1. Don't be afraid of failure; embrace it. It is a gift of growth. It is hard and humbling, but it makes us better. 2. Be humble enough to own your mistakes and give grace to those who make mistakes around you.

Hoffer Plastics has been around for over 60 years and is a world-wide industry leader. What leadership skills have you learned from your dad and grandfather that you incorporate daily into your routine?

Our company was founded by our grandparents in 1953. They were very simple people who believed in doing things the right way and treating people fairly. They taught our family humility and the importance of serving and stewardship. Our grandfather led our company with a servant's heart. He cared deeply and intrinsically about our employees, customers, and community. He was truly a master at connection, and people need to feel connection. Our father, who has been running the company for over a decade, leads with great intention and discipline. I have learned from his steadfast decision making. He seeks to understand first while using our core values to drive his decision making.

You are an amazing business leader, wife, community liaison and mother. What are the top three habits you structure your life around to be so successful in so many areas?

1.Gratitude. I thank God continuously for my blessed life. 2. Put your air mask on before assisting others. If I am not intentional about taking care of myself, I cannot truly give my best to my loved ones. I have worked at making sure to carve out time for working out, to eat a balanced diet, and to get a decent night's rest. 3. I am intentional about finding fun in everything I do. I have to laugh – it is like oxygen to me.

What has been your greatest failure? What did you learn from it?

I moved to Nashville after college and recorded a CD (which makes me sound so ancient). A very close, committed friend moved down with me to support my project and do creative work for my album. I let other people in the process have too much ownership in the process, and her name was left off the credits for the project. I missed it completely before we went to print. She was understandably devastated. I was so focused on me that I missed giving credit where credit was due. It still haunts me how selfish I was in that moment and reminds me every day to give people deserved acknowledgment. There is very little in life that we can do by ourselves. People need to know that their work, time, etc, matters.

What is your favorite quote of all time?

"My command is this: Love each other as I have loved you." John 15:12 NIV

I have known you for over 30 years, and you always smile with everything you do. What is your secret?

I don't think there is any secret. It is mindset really. I choose to be positive and try to be intentional about smiling. We live in a world that is so full of negativity- choose kindness. See the difference it might make to smile at people or hold the door for someone. Everyone is fighting a battle of some sort and maybe a smile can make a difference in their day.

What do you do when you feel overwhelmed?

Lots of different things. I sing. I pray and read Scripture. I also have found that intentional, meditative breathing can calm my thoughts and demeanor.

What is your definition of success?

Personally – success to me is making others know that I care about them. Success is so subjective. I certainly would not define it by anything material in nature. I would say putting forth your best efforts at whatever you are striving to achieve and being honest.

CHAPTER 20

Listen More Than You Speak

"Most people don't listen with the intent to understand; they listen with the intent to reply."

- Stephen Covey

When I was a kid, there was one saying that I most remembered from my grandma: "You have two ears and one mouth. Use your ears wisely."

I never really understood what she meant by that. I never asked and she never went into detail. However, a couple decades later, that quote has come full circle with so much truth for me. As a doctor, I think the number one thing that I have had to learn has been the art of listening. I have had thousands of patients over the years, and almost every single one of them has given me their diagnosis without me ever physically touching them. When we take the time to actively listen to what people have to say, they fill our minds with all the pieces of the puzzle needed to make our next move. About 90% of being a doctor is listening, and the final 10% is physical examination or treatment. There has never been a time more important than now as listening seems like a lost art.

Social media, texting, and the world of superficial communication devices have replaced the days of face-to-face interaction. Now, when we meet someone in person, we forget how to truly communicate. People have forgotten the basics of listening and, instead, they treat conversation as a competitive sport. Whoever talks the most, talks the loudest, gives the most opinions, and dominates the conversation wins. Think honestly about some of the most recent conversations you have had. How many of them did you really invest in the other person? Or are you mainly concerned with getting your own view across? So let's go back in time a little and revisit what it means to be an active listener.

Active listening is the communication art which requires the listener to fully concentrate, understand, remember, and respond to what the other party said. The hardest part of that equation is to concentrate. When we concentrate completely on what the other party is saying, we are giving them the respect that they deserve. We are fully invested in understanding what they are trying to say. The opposite, which is done more often, is pretending to listen but consciously thinking about what you're going to say next. How are you supposed to concentrate, understand, remember, and respond to anything when you aren't fully engaged in listening to them in the first place?

Years ago, I took a course on leadership coaching. I was so excited to learn the foundations of leadership and how to talk someone through excellence in their life. Guess what RULE #1 was? Listening! A great leader or coach becomes great by listening more than they speak. They ignore the selfish, ego-driven need to hear themselves talk. Instead, they invest energy into those around them to be better. When we engage in active listening, we make a commitment to ourselves not to speak without thinking. A truly authentic response deserves a short pause to formulate that thought. If your response is immediate, or even before the other party finishes, then you are not fully engaged in the conversation and your sole purpose is your own agenda.

Abe Lincoln had a great quote that revolves around the premise of listening more than you speak. He said, "Better to remain silent and be thought a fool than to speak and remove all doubt." Sometimes when we speak without properly formulating our response, we are jumping to conclusions. We are not thinking out an intelligent next move, and we are saying whatever comes to mind. I support saying what is on your mind, but it is still important to take a second and formulate that thought based on the context. Once it comes out of your mouth, you can't take it back.

Speaking is an absolute gift filled with emotions, feelings, and ideas. Speaking gives us the power to create change in this world, bigger than we ever thought was possible. Speaking allows us to connect with an audience and grow a community who believe that they, too, can "Make It Count!" However, speaking can sometimes be a filler — and it limits the amount we can learn. When we speak, we are usually regurgitating ideas we already know. We are sharing knowledge we already have. When we listen, and I mean truly listen, we learn something new.

Benefits of listening:

1. **Knowledge** - When we listen we are actively taking in information instead of processing our next move. Everytime I go to a seminar, meeting, class or speaking engagement I go in with the intent to be fully present in my listening. If I am preoccupied with tomorrow or already think what I am going to hear won't be good, then I have failed myself. In every opportunity we have to open those two ears to the potential of gaining something we didn't know before.
2. **Trust** - In meaningful conversations with others, there is nothing more detrimental to gaining their trust than to seem uninterested, somewhere else, or constantly interrupting the other person. Listening shows the other person that you are 100 percent there for them and that you value their time and voice.
3. **Productive Response** - Like the Abe Lincoln quote above, sometimes it's the best to pursue the silent route then to speak so fast as to be thought a fool. When our mind fully takes in the knowledge we gather from a conversation, we can then fully process what our productive response should be. This productive response then builds up the trust again.
4. **Confidence** - When you participate in active listening, your confidence immediately improves. The reason is that you are more engaged in the

conversation, you are more engaged in next steps, more engaged in the potential our life presents, and more engaged in furthering the success of our community. People will seek you out for what you bring to the table. Your community will grow around their belief in you. This new found love, compassion and encouragement has an immediate impact on making you a better person. A better person equals increased confidence.

5. **Uncover opportunities** - When you focus on being better, when you focus on active listening and you focus on being present time focused opportunities have an uncanny way of always showing up on your doorstep. Most conversations will present you with opportunities should you pay attention. Conversations have the ability to present you with the opportunity to be a good friend, to help someone in need, to teach and be taught, and even the opportunity to identify the next great unicorn in the making.

One thing that always reminds me to focus on listening is traveling everywhere with either a notebook or the notes section opened up on my phone. The amount of notes on my phone alone could write their own novel. Always having some type of note or writing device in close range gives us two advantages. The first is having a source to take down the knowledge that others share with us. Every conversation can provide us with a new way of thinking, a new approach to fitness, or a new habit that we never thought would apply to our world. The second benefit, previously mentioned in this book, is that writing frees up the monkey mind. Sometimes the monkey business in our head becomes the focus of our conversations which can get us in trouble and off track. Writing down these thoughts ahead of time, or after a conversation, gets the monkey business out and onto paper. Then we can read what we wrote, analyze its value, and decide what we should do from there.

Active listening is not something that we are automatically good at. Some of the best interviewers in the world are great not just because they ask good questions, but because they are focused on the present-time and in the moment. They are authentically driven to understand the individual they are connecting with. Their questions may be great, but it's really their ability to listen that has allowed them to make every interview count.

Make It Count Foundations

1. Active listening helps form a solid communication base, but it requires practice. The first thing you can do in a conversation is to take a moment after someone is done talking to think of a response you would like to share that you believe will be powerful.

2. When we speak, we are just repeating what we already know. Listening allows us to expand our knowledge base by learning something new.

3. Listening helps with speaking and vice versa. When we listen, we formulate powerful responses we can be proud of.

4. Listening limits the amount of interruption that occurs, which allows for trust to build between two people. When we consistently interrupt a conversation, we are essentially telling the other person that we don't value their feedback. When you let someone share their concept, you can then come back with your response which helps build trust and respect.

5. Never leave home without a notepad or the notes on your phone ready. Taking notes while listening is a way to remember the pearls of wisdom shared. It also allows us to get thoughts out of our head before we sit down to talk with someone.

Make It Counter: Shaun Smithson

A native Texan, Shaun moved to Maryland during his years in the United States Air Force Honor Guard. He met his wife, Jen, during his third year of enlistment. They married shortly after and currently live in Highland, MD with their 4 kids. Throughout his life, Shaun has coached kids in baseball, basketball, and soccer. The joy of seeing a kid discover a passion for playing and learning more about themselves on and off the field drives Shaun to seek new and engaging ways to motivate every kid he coaches. Professionally, Shaun serves as the State Director for Maryland FCA (Fellowship Christian Athletes) where he considers it a great honor to combine his love of coaching with his love of God and the love of sport through his work.

What are your top three habits you consistently perform?

I have found that my habits change often, but there are three areas of focus that I have found must be a part of any routine for me to maintain joy and productivity.

1. **People** - I love building relationships with people who share a common desire and drive. I continually try to put myself in places where I am joined with others to strive towards a common goal. These situations happen through work, through competition, through coaching, through volunteering, and beyond.

2. **Purpose** - I love when I finish a day having accomplished something that will impact someone else's tomorrow in a positive way. The habit that comes with this is planning ahead. If I don't spend time preparing for the people I will see at the next meeting or practice, the meetings become a matter of routine rather than purpose.

3. **Prayer** - Pursuing a purpose that matters with people you care about can be exhausting and sometimes frustrating when things don't work out the way you had hoped. A constant habit of prayer allows me to give God the things that I cannot control in order for me to stay focused on handling the things that I can.

On a daily basis, you have the absolute privilege of working with the next generation of leadership through Fellowship of Christian Athletes. What have you noticed is a positive characteristic these kids have in common?

I think there are two things that stand out about these athletes who excel on and off the field: The first is **that they have 1 or more people who believe in them and support them on and off the field**. This is something that we all need and is definitely an area where I can give you, Jake Oergel, a huge thank you for the impact that you have had on me as a coach. Your constant encouragement to both your daughter and to me, while I coached your daughter, and even today when she no longer plays directly on my team, has given me the fuel to succeed. The second is that they understand that their ability to play is a gift that not everyone has been given, giving them a sense of **gratitude and humility**.

What is the most difficult decision that you have had to make in your life?

I think I have to go back to late high school for this one. When I was around 16 or 17, I made the decision to tell my dad that I did not think I wanted to stay with the family automotive business that he and my Grandpa started. I think my dad knew that I would more than likely not go in that direction before I did, but the decision and conversation still came with the fear that I might be letting him down. True to his form, if he was disappointed, he never told me. He knew I had a desire to find out what else was out there for me and he supported me in that decision.

What do the words "Make It Count" mean to you?

"Make It Count" means making someone else's tomorrow better through the things I invest my time, talent, and treasure in today. On a higher level, it means helping others clarify and accomplish the dreams that God is giving them so that they can find the joy that He intended for them.

I have seen you transform kids, both physically and mentally over the years, and provide them with a foundation that will help them become amazing individuals. Where does the passion to dedicate your time to these kids come from?

3 John 1:4- There is no greater joy than hearing that your children are walking in the truth. The word for children is not a word of definition but a word of opportunity. All who you have the opportunity to influence fall into this category. I couldn't agree more with John. Watching any one of the kids or adults I have had the privilege to coach learn more about who they are, who God is, and what they were put on earth to accomplish brings joy like nothing else. And joy is the fuel of passion!

What is one thing that has had the most impact on your life?

Aside from God's love and the fact that he never gives up on me no matter how often I stubbornly pursue my own plans, it has been the men and women one or two generations ahead of me who have chosen to invest their time and energy into mentoring and encouraging me. My parents and grandparents are just the beginning. My Uncle Danny coached my baseball and football team even though he didn't have a kid of his own on the team. Grady and Opal Smith invited me into their kitchen for a cup of iced tea, a fried apple pie, and good conversation more times than I can count. Todd invited me on the ski trip where God finally grabbed my attention. Larry & Josh Moody believed in me and patiently spoke truth to me when I still lacked the humility it took to listen and learn. The list goes on and on and reminds me that I am nothing more than a conduit taking the good things that I have been taught and passing them on to others who will pass them on to others still.

What is your definition of success?

- Daily- Make someone else's tomorrow better.
- Weekly/Monthly- Learn more about leadership, love, and God. Invest what I have been given in my family, friends, and community in a way that makes tomorrow better.
- Lifetime- See my children walking in the truth about who they are, who God is, and what he wants from them during their short stay on this planet.

If you could put one saying on a billboard, what would it say and why?

Invest in tomorrow by coaching today! (Right next to a picture of one of my teams!) I would also include this quote below the big text above if I could get away with two sayings. *"A coach will impact more people in one year than the average person will in an entire lifetime."* - Billy Graham

CHAPTER 21

Indomitable Will

"Strength does not come from physical capacity. It comes from an indomitable will."

- Mahatma Gandhi

The perfect starting point for this chapter is with the definition of "indomitable." The word is defined as "impossible to subdue or defeat." I think we can all agree that life is not linear, but is instead full of peaks and valleys. Life has ups and downs, successes and failures, love and loss, strengths and weaknesses, moments of creative genius and moments of blank slates, and an uncertainty about what will happen next. The key through all of these ebbs and flows is not to give up and not to invite defeat into your life.

We need to create a strong aversion to quitting. Do you know that anyone can give up? That it's the easiest thing for someone to do? It doesn't take much to quit something. You don't like your job? Walk away. You think the Crossfit workout is too hard? Leave. You don't like your meal at the new restaurant? Never come back. If you are challenged in life and you don't like it, then you can choose something else to do. It's very easy to decide that something is not for you. With the limited time we have in life, quitting might seem like the best option. The problem is that you will never be challenged to grow.

Quitting will never give you the chance to expose the person you are deep inside. This is where the indomitable will comes into play. As Gandhi said, "Strength doesn't come from muscle but comes from the person who refuses to give up." Those with extreme success and those whom you admire on a daily basis both have one thing in common: an unquestionable will to succeed. They know the yellow brick road will be filled with distractions, but it is the distractions that allow each character to learn about their weaknesses. Like failure, weakness is not a negative word. Both are words that we need to understand in order to apply them to our lives.

Make your weakness a strength. Turn that failure into a success. Don't quit when times get tough.

One of my best friends, Eduardo, has had every opportunity in life to quit. But it has been his indomitable will to succeed that has kept him moving forward. Eduardo's life mantra is: "It's hard to beat the person who never gives up!" Eduardo has not only crushed it professionally in the United States, after growing up in Argentina, but he has also maintained a daily mission to improve the lives of everyone around him. He has been an Ironman Triathlon training partner of mine for years. About five years ago, he was out for a run and collapsed mid-way through. His heart had stopped beating, due to an undiagnosed heart condition. Fortunately, EMT's were able to get to him quickly enough to save his life.

The next six months were riddled with doctor visits, with uncertainty about his future and his ability to do the thing he loved most. I'm not sure that even with the "Make It Count" principles that I have fought hard to live by, that I could have held up the positive mindset that he had from day one. His mission, or his indomitable will, was not to give up and to keep fighting — as it's hard to beat the man who never gives up.

When your indomitable will is strong, then no matter how you feel — tired, upset, depressed, angry, confused, irritated, or hopeless — you will keep moving forward, no matter what. That progressive motion creates such a momentum that you start to develop positive habits in your life, forcing you to always move forward. There is plenty of opportunity for growth in a moment of fatigue. When you are fatigued — mentally, physically, spiritually — and there doesn't seem to be any moment of relief coming, then the will to succeed forces you to swim faster.

Years ago, I ran a 50-mile trail race. At mile 35, I was about ready to throw in the towel. I was mentally exhausted, my ankle was ready to explode, and I questioned my motivation for everything. It was at this point that I remembered how my daughters had each written the notes that were in my pocket. I thought if I was ready to quit, then what would it matter if I stopped running to read those letters. The love, confidence, passion, and honesty within them reminded me of why I do everything I do. My will has always been to be the best version of myself. I realized, at mile 35, that quitting was never an option for me. But I questioned whether or not I was ready to level up the person that I was.

Was I willing to dig deep for another 15 miles? To not only find out what I was made of, but also to do exactly what the title of my book says and "MAKE IT COUNT?!" Crossing that finish line wasn't about the relief of it being over. Crossing that finish line was a rebirth of a new level of accomplishment that I now believed I was capable of. My will to succeed was always there, I just needed to change my state of mind in that moment. I needed to realize that it is through those moments of struggle that the real version of my new self is born.

All of the principles in this book have led to developing the indomitable will. When we have purpose in action and we know that all our actions are geared toward "Making It Count," then our indomitable will becomes our bulletproof armor. When we have an indomitable will, we are able to encompass the "powerful three" — acceptance, state change and growth mindset.

Acceptance - One of the biggest factors in any growth pattern is accepting what is going on. When we accept that peaks and valleys, ups and downs and success and failures are part of the journey, we accept that they will come and that we will be ready. When we accept that the road ahead will be a rocky one, we know, without a doubt, that our will to succeed will plow through the difficult challenges. Accept that everything will happen within a day and know that your indomitable will prevails all the time.

State Change – Human emotions are a beast which are hard to tame at times. One second you can be riding high and the next you can feel like "why me?" This is what makes life great. If nothing changed or nothing challenged you, then you're either hiding in a closet or dead. When the times get tough, like my 50-miler did, and you're questioning why, the easiest thing to do sometimes is force yourself to make a state change. Smile, laugh, talk to a neighbor about something you love or go for a run. Force yourself, in that moment, to make a drastic, immediate change to your state. It won't always be easy and at times you will fail but usually if you are having a tough day and you do something positive, you set yourself up for a better next chapter.

Growth Mindset - There are only two types of mindsets. You can either be in a fixed mindset or a growth mindset. Its either one or the other but never both. When our indomitable will is strong, our growth mindset multiples because we are looking at each action, event, activity or priority with the mindset that something good is going to happen. This forces the brain to get creative and search through your catalogue of experiences to decide how to proceed. Growth mindset is the best mindset we can put forward because it's a mindset of better times, of becoming your best version and it's a mindset that is the fuel for an indomitable will.

Make It Count Foundations

1. Remember that strength doesn't come from anything other than your will to keep moving forward, no matter the obstacles.

2. Life is not a linear process. There will be peaks and valleys, but understanding that allows us to confidently build our willpower so we are ready.

3. There are many personality traits incorporated into an indomitable will, but most revolve around having an unquestionable will to succeed: having an insatiable appetite to continue growing.

4. Remember the quote "It's hard to beat a man who never gives up."? Keeping that mantra in your head will help you to focus on continued forward momentum instead of losing steam to the sidetrackers of life.

5. Fixed mindset or a growth mindset. The book, *Mindset* is a gift that keeps giving every time I read it. The author does an amazing job of depicting why a growth mindset is so important for everything we do. Having that growth mindset helps you build an indomitable will but is also necessary to always "Make It Count."

Make It Counter: Greg Karr

I was born in 1957 and lived as a young child in Chicago before moving to the Northern Suburbs in the early 1960's to a home my parents maintained for over 50 years. I was second in line of a family of four children, two sisters and a brother. We were a typical middle-class family. My father went to work and my mother was home to take care of all of us. Later, my mother re-entered the work force. Having four children with seven post high school degrees put a strain on family finances. Much of the social, political and family experiences of the 60's and 70's shaped our lives in such a way that the stories and memories I share with my contemporaries sound very similar. We had one black and white TV, and the fun we had was the fun we made. The statement: "Just be home for dinner" was a daily mantra. We played sports, participated in Scouting, family vacations, church, summer camp and had jobs at a very early age. My first job was cutting lawns in the neighborhood and I had a job up until the day I retired. I had almost every job imaginable from caddy, dishwasher, cook, bartender, landscaper to bookkeeper in a bank. My friends and I had our share of adventures we would never share with our parents (none involved the police or jail time). Surviving that period of adolescence was the first success of my life. I was very fortunate to be able to attend one of the finest public high schools in the country. The expectation of attending college was the norm for almost my entire graduating class.

When I was young, I always enjoyed making things, taking things apart and attempting to fix any broken item around the house. Working with my hands was a skill I excelled at, it was natural that I was very much drawn to the career of a dentist. The field of dentistry requires a unique combination of human qualities, such as intelligence, fine motor control, artistic abilities, personal communication and management skills. I had always marveled at the skill and precision of my family dentist, so, at the age of 12, I decided it was for me.

I have always been a planner: my goals, year by year were scribbled in the margins of my school notebooks. Graduate high school in 1975, attend a four year college, 1979. Get a degree that would allow me to apply to dental school and graduate, 1983. Work and retire by the time I was 60.

I graduated high school in 1975 and attended and graduated from Purdue University with a Bachelor Degree in Biology and a minor in Chemistry in 1979. I then went on to attend Northwestern University Dental School and graduated in 1983. Then I completed an advanced residency program in General Dentistry at the Veterans Hospital in Minneapolis Minnesota. So far so good, planning paid off.

In the final two years of dental school I met my wife, Lynda. To this day she laughs at me for this, but when I met her I knew she was the one for me. The only problem was she was not on board with my plan. It took some convincing, and some imaginable dates. Three years later we were married in 1984. We had hopes and dreams just like most young couples. One of my life long dreams was to build my own home. Over the years I developed a passion for woodworking and all things related to building, construction and landscaping. Early on in our lives we were able to purchase a lot to build our future home. We built a home in 1992 where we continue to live today.

After my residency, I returned to the Chicago area and began working for a dentist in the town of Elgin, Illinois. Lynda, a graphic designer, worked in Evanston at Northwestern University designing their publications. In 1988, we were given the shocking news that the dentist I was working for had been diagnosed with Parkinson's disease and would be retiring. Not in the plan. This required a big decision: buy the practice I was working at or look for a new position elsewhere. We decided to purchase the dental practice. In 1989, after it was all said and done, I became the owner of a very busy dental practice, a mountain of debt, and $63 in our checking account. I worked very hard to be the best I could and to elevate those around me. We had a caring and compassionate office, a place very much like a family. I retired in 2016 and if you add the total numbers of years my six employees worked for me, it was over one-hundred.

In 1990, we celebrated the birth of our first daughter Alexandra, followed by daughter number two, Kendall, in 1992, and, finally, our son, Gavin, in 1995. We are so proud of our children pursuing careers they love in hopes of making our world a better place. Now we enter a new chapter in our lives as grandparents. Alexandra is expecting her first child in March, 2019.

Lynda and I shared a full life raising our children and being their guiding light in their lives. We showed them the wonders of the world in which we live. We traveled, exposed them to art, the outdoors, learning and giving back. Sure we had our ups and downs, anyone who says they haven't surely is not being honest with you. I wish I had heard the "Make It Count" motto earlier, because I think for me it is kind of the way I have lived. For those who live the good life, one's expectations would be that it should go on, especially for a planner, like myself.

In April of 2015 I was finishing up my last patient, casually talking at the end of the appointment when the dental mirror I had in my hand slipped and fell to the floor. I had thought I had a good grip on the handle. Maybe, I was just tired. I brushed it off. Went home to relax and work around the yard on my long weekend. However, by Monday my left hand was no longer functioning; it was paralyzed. By chance, I had an appointment already scheduled with my physician. After examining me, she scheduled me to meet with a neurologist that afternoon. To be safe, she ordered a CAT scan of my head. After the test I was asked to return to her office. My doctor and I have been friends and colleagues for over thirty years. When I returned to the office I could sense the mood had changed. She took me to an exam room to inform me I had a brain tumor. This was one of those, "My life changed forever" moments. All of the questions that instantly entered my head seemed overwhelming. In a week and a half I went from living a normal life to fighting for that life. We all hoped the tumor was something not so catastrophic, yet given all I knew about brain tumors, my age, and the circumstances which the tumor presented itself, I knew it was Glioblastoma. Glioblastoma is a very aggressive non-curable tumor that often claims the lives of those unfortunate enough to be afflicted with it in 12-18 months. The following week I was at Northwestern Memorial Hospital preparing to have brain surgery. Due to the proximity of the tumor to the part of the brain that controls my left hand it was necessary to perform the surgery while I was awake. That is the time in your life where you have to have the utmost trust in your medical team. I came through the surgery with amazingly good results. The journey was just beginning. Those who have said that battling cancer is not a sprint but a marathon were absolutely correct.

The hopes of a lower grade, less aggressive tumor were not realized. My diagnosis was confirmed. I had Glioblastoma Grade 4 brain cancer. I only spent two days in the hospital, but now faced a treatment schedule that included radiation and chemotherapy, followed by 12 months of more chemotherapy, finishing up in August, 2016.

I did return to work, but we decided the stress of continuing to work was not in my best interest. We decided to sell my dental practice and take an early retirement. Not in the Plan. Even when the absolute worst things creep into one's life, "Make it Count", is a motto that can often be one's salvation. Faced with the prospect of having less than two years to live, we decided to make every day count - to be with family, travel, meet new people. I must say we have embraced this to the fullest. We still continue to make plans and to look to the future. My cancer has not returned, now approaching four years, which seems improbable. Many people touched by the same disease as me have since passed away, and for that I am sad. I wish they all had the gift of time I have been given. It does something to you, to be told your plan might not be the life you lead. No one knows for certain if they will have many tomorrows. I look at everyday things differently. Things that I found annoying or objectionable, I don't find they elicit the same response now. I wonder if everyone were told they have a year to live, would they embrace the "Make It Count" motto? I think if they experience a life of making every day count our world would be a better place.

What one thing has had the biggest impact on your life?

I feel that being a parent has had the biggest impact on my life. It is a tremendous responsibility to have and care for a new life in this world yet, it is the greatest gift one can give. You nurture and teach another human being to love, live, and prosper. As a parent you get to see young minds and hearts discover an amazing world. With that you witness the potential they have to impact future events, to be part of something bigger than all of us.

A couple of years ago, you were diagnosed with a glioblastoma (brain cancer). What have you learned about yourself during the process of treatment, staying so positive and never giving up?

Having been handed a medical diagnosis of such devastating consequences, one never knows how you might respond. Give up, and spiral downward, or fight? I chose to fight, with every ounce of courage and strength, to hopefully ward off a very uncertain future. I also learned this is something one does not do alone. You never quite know how many people you have in your corner until something like this happens. On a daily basis it might not be apparent, but, once it becomes necessary to gather your support network, you will be astonished by the number of people who care.

What are three non-negotiables in your life? Have they changed since the diagnosis? Or have they always been the same three?

Love, Knowledge, and Integrity are my non-negotiable components of my personal life. I am sure these exact three were not what I would have said when I was young. They have developed over a period of time. These are the ones I hold close to this day. If you want to integrate "Make It Count" in you daily life, I could not imagine these three attributes not being part of how your life.

What is your favorite quote and why?

"Success is not final, failure is not fatal, it is the courage to continue that counts" - Winston Churchill.

Nobody in this world is perfect and no one has all the answers. We will all experience success and failure. How you handle both of these will determine your character.

What is your favorite book? Maybe one you have gifted the most?

The Last Lecture by Randy Pausch

Randy Pausch was a professor at Carnegie Mellon University. It is a long standing tradition at Carnegie that when a professor is retiring, they give a "last lecture." This presentation may include a synopsis of their body of work, an important idea or concept, or something they feel is essential to share with the world. Unfortunately for Randy, his last lecture was not given at the zenith of a long career. It was given because he was a middle-aged man, with a young family, and he was dying of pancreatic cancer. In his brief career as a computer engineer, he worked with some of the most notable computer companies and taught many young minds to think and embrace the future. His book was published in April 2008. Randy passed away in July of that year. I read it, made sure my kids read it, and often recommended it to others. It would be less than seven years before I realized I was facing a diagnosis with the same potential outcome as Randy. I had not forgotten about this book, but as life moves on, we shift focus, and encounter different interests. When given a diagnosis that often results in living only 12-18 months, you often reflect on things that had an impact on you. I think this book had a large impact on me as to how to approach life and the possible result of a life ending too soon. A fact of serendipity is that his entire book has the thread of "Make It Count" woven through it.

What do you do when you feel overwhelmed?

I may not be the best at giving advice on handling feelings of stress or being overwhelmed. I don't feel in the past I had engaged in the most healthy response to life's stressors. I tended to turn inward and get quiet, not sharing my concerns or struggles with others around me. I have been getting better at how I approach struggles as they present themselves. It is always a work in progress. I have learned over the years to engage in a greater breath of active response to stress. Speaking with someone (a loved one, a professional, a friend) is always better than my former actions or lack thereof. Regular physical activity also helps tremendously with stress, something most of us could use more of. Having a solid plan and executing it to the best of one's ability is a great addition to a complete and whole life. The outcome may not be the one envisioned, but it is much better than no plan at all.

What piece of advice would you give to a younger version of yourself?

The advice I would give to a younger me would be:

Do with less, stop, explore, and learn. What we all have every day on earth is a gift. I have done this to a degree. However, you get caught up in the trappings of life, and tend to lose direction. We often need reminders to show us a path. None of us know how long we have on this planet. "Make It Count." I know this may seem cliché to say those things but being told you could die in 18 months has a way of focusing you.

If there was a definition for "Make It Count," your picture would be the example. What do the words "Make It Count" mean to you?

"Make It Count" is something that in retrospect, I had incorporated in my daily life, but never put a moniker to it. I never really thought about naming it, but I could not think of a better way to live. What it means to me now is to live with a definitive purpose, whether faced with a large or small task. Never pass up an opportunity to learn, love, grow. Be engaged and improve the lives of those around you.

CHAPTER 22

Memento Mori

"Dream like you'll live forever. Live like you'll die today."

- James Dean

I contemplated not writing this chapter as I thought the meaning of its name might seem too sad to include in a book about developing a more proactive lifestyle. However, I also thought about how living such a lifestyle is all about embracing "memento mori" itself.

If you're not familiar, the term is Latin for "remember that you will die." When I first saw it while reading my favorite book, *The Obstacle is the Way* by Ryan Holiday, my first thought was what might it be like to live a life centered around the idea that we will someday die. I think we often get caught up in life's race and we forget that we are not invincible. We are not an "Avenger" character, sent from another world to protect everyone. We *are* living, breathing people who will reach a point in time when our lives come to a close. For most of us, that time is an unknown.

This is where Memento Mori and "Make It Count" cross paths. These concepts try to help us live for the moment, based on the principle to not settle for less than the best. All the principles in this book have their own different meanings, and they offer many different examples of how to make the most of any given situation. This particular chapter just flips the switch, which allows us to venture into what I like to call "death awareness." This does not mean living a life in fear that we will die, but rather living a life in certainty that each waking hour is a gift waiting to be met with success. We are constantly surrounded by things that are dying.

Every Sunday, my family goes grocery shopping together. We come home, unload the groceries, and I always set the bananas on the counter. No matter how many we buy or how quickly we eat them, by the end of the week there are always a couple of them left on the counter — black, wilted, and filled with fruit flies. I always stop to look at those bananas and compare them to our weeks as humans. Each day that we wake up, we are one step closer to the end. We have one less opportunity to make an impact on our legacy. It is one less chance for us to decide to quit thinking about our dreams and to go out in pursuit of them instead.

There are a few guest writers in this book who have battled cancer and, for now, they've won. The one consistent thing that I have noticed within each of them is their ability to consider each day a blessing. They might never have heard the words Memento Mori, but it is that definition that seems to have inspired them to fight for everything they have and more. Bad things will happen to us over time - that is a given. Our perspectives will be challenged, and life will seem extremely unfair. We will all have a different response to the events that take place in our lives, but what will affect everything is our perspective.

We first have to avoid getting too lost in what's happening around us. This blinds us from seeing exactly what it is that we need to do in the next second. We need to have principles in place, along with the belief that better times are right around the corner. This will push us over the mountain when we feel like we are stumbling backwards. Principles tend to arise best from life's experiences - from what the journey has done for us.

My whole life I have fought for my dad's time. Unfortunately, each and every time I would make headway, alcoholism would stick out its ugly head and win. I felt let down and disappointed. The frustration was deep and I couldn't get myself to understand the meaning that this had in my life: one person's struggle to choose family and life's gifts over such a powerful drug. My dream was that one day my dad would wake up to realize that sharing opportunities with his family could triumph over a lifelong addiction. Life seemed more of a hindrance to him, and it was like he had no principle meaning for each day that passed. Missed birthdays, missed sporting events, missed medical emergencies, and overall missed experiences became the norm. My goal was always to find the meaning behind these events happening in my life. Someone from whom I so craved love and attention could not seem to give it. There was no cry for help from him but a constant insistence that nothing was wrong.

It wasn't until I had kids of my own that I found my trigger for growth. My reminder that there is more to life than the bottle came in the form of three beautiful girls. I now have a chance to take my frustration and invest that energy into providing better lives for my kids. Here was my golden ticket to leaving a legacy in my kid's lives — that their dad was always there, always willing to help, and always part of their support system. My Memento Mori came in the form of a need to maximize every second with my kids, because any time missed felt like becoming a father I didn't want to be. I raised my game for living in the moment, and I decided that the only way to attack life was through the mentality I have laid out in this book.

The given that life will eventually come to an end doesn't scare me one bit, because I am fully engaged with the promise that I will waste no time waiting for opportunity to find me. Opportunity comes through our actions, and those actions get dusty when left on the shelf. I keep my shelf empty by always going deep into what I want to do in this life.

This summer, I had a deep conversation with a close friend of mine — about death. I asked, "Would you be happy with your life if you died tomorrow?" You'd be amazed to find out what that simple question can do to motivate you to think about the things you want to accomplish versus what you haven't accomplished yet. We need to stop avoiding conversations about death, because it's exactly the kind of talk that can free us from our fears. It's exactly that kind of conversation that can open up our bucket list for life and push us to pursue those opportunities that we keep pushing off until the next year.

Remember that living a life with the knowledge we will die doesn't have to be a negative experience. Experience and definition are always about perspective, and the following points bring perspective to living a life focused only on today:

Smile — There is nothing more powerful to your daily activities than smiling. Not only does a smile have the ability to change your perspective on an event, but it also has the ability to bring instant energy to any event. A smile brings life to any party, and it doesn't take much to produce. When we smile, we are letting life know that we are fully engaging in our journey. The counter arguments are always, "What if I don't want to smile?", "What if I am in a bad mood?", "What if something is going on that doesn't deserve a smile?" I wholeheartedly understand that life is not always going to be unicorns and rainbows, but we still have the capacity to make sure each day that we try to spend most of our time with a smile.

Constantly Add Value — Each day, I write down three things that I know I can add value to my life. I might not get the chance on certain days to perform a valuable task. But if it's in my mind's eye, then I know I am formulating an other-people focused mindset. If I, instead, focus on pouting that life isn't fair and struggle to find "the point," then that is exactly the type of day I will have. Our days are hard when we become too self-focused. When we reach out to help others, then our opportunities expand exponentially. When we are searching to add value to the journeys of others, we are focusing on getting the most out of our own journey, too.

Help Focus On What's Important — Nothing is more of a waste of time than when you focus on things that don't really matter in the big picture. As I have repeated, time is the only commodity that we can't make more of. When a moment is gone, it can't be replaced. Why waste those moments stressing over items that really don't matter? Be it opinions (whether or not a shirt looks good), "what ifs," or the unnecessary approval of others — each of these have the ability to distract you from what's actually important. Don't waste your time living someone else's dream because you were too concerned about what they think. Focus on what is important to you. If it helps, regularly write down what matters most to you and focus on crushing those points.

Urgency — Be urgent, but don't stress. For two years, I stressed over writing this book. I have always wanted to write a book, but I let the less important things get in the way of my dreams. Don't wait until tomorrow to do what could be done today. Don't wait until you're on your deathbed wishing you would have chased every dream that crossed your path. Pretend each day is your deathbed and attack your goals with urgency and determination. Dream big, but wake up and make sure that those dreams are turning into a reality....TODAY!

Be Present — Stop focusing on tomorrow, next week, next month, and next year. Moments in the future are not here yet, nor are they guaranteed to get here. Why waste an ounce of energy on something that might not happen? I understand having 1-year, 5-year and 10-year goals as an example of looking into the future. And I do somewhat agree with that process. However, use that macro thinking to process your micro today. If your goal is to be the vice president of your company in 5 years, then stop stressing over anything beyond today and simply focus on what you can do to support that goal right now. The same is true when the day is over - you can move onto the next day, fully present. What's in the past is in the past. We can fully absorb any and all lessons, but we can't stress over events that are over. They are finished, so we need to move on and stop wasting unnecessary time on things we can't redo.

Live By Your Mission — One great way to live in the present is to live by your mission. At the end of the book, you can find my personal mission statement. The process to develop one of your own is simple. I chose a picture of a setting that means the world to me. It's my comfort spot - a place where I feel like life is perfect. I then filled in statements relating to what I want to accomplish in my life, each and everyday. The purpose of this is similar to a company's mission statement — it is your personal idea for how you want to live your life. It's your code for what's important to you, and it's the metrics you apply to everything you do. This is a powerful tool that has helped me re-focus numerous times, on what is most important for me and how I should spend my time.

Spread Gratitude — Grateful people are more forgiving in life. They hold themselves more accountable, and communication is of the utmost importance to them. Sharing gratitude becomes their mission. Gratitude allows us to live in abundance, and to escape from the opinions, attacks, and attempts from others to bring us down. Gratitude makes us stronger because we are truly living out our life in a way that allows us to understand that each moment is a gift. Grateful people stand strong in their principles and beliefs, knowing that they will not let others steal their joy. When we don't let others steal our energy, we have more energy to share. When we have more to share, we are living in the moment and understand that the only way to attack our day is to "Make It Count."

What if you were told you only had 24 hours to live? What would you do? What would become most important to you? What things would suddenly seem to be a waste of your time, thinking or doing?

While I certainly hope you have more than 24 hours to live, in reality we actually have no idea how much time we have. Our end point is unknown, but we *do* know that someday this incredible journey will be over. So, why not live each day like its your last? I realize you have to work, but find a job you absolutely love. I realize you have chores to do around the house, so make them fun with some dancing and music. I realize it might be raining outside and you love the sun, but go run around in the rain like you did when you were a kid. I realize you have to drive your kids all over the earth for practices, but look at it as a gift of time spent with the ones you love. Everything we do during our day is filtered through our perspective. My wife always says, "If you don't like something, then do something about it immediately."

So what would you do if you only had 24 hours to live?

Make It Count Foundations

1. What do you feel when you hear the words Memento Mori ("remember you will die.")?

2. Having death awareness doesn't make you a negative thinker but allows you to be aware of how delicate and fragile our time is and allows you to have more of an impact.

3. Bad things will happen, you will be challenged, life will seem unfair. The key is to not get caught up in the moment and instead develop a perspective on what's important to you.

4. How you spend your days is how you spend your life. Spend a week writing down how you spent your days. Similar to a food journal for a week. If we write down our actions, thoughts and ideas throughout a day we might be able to analyze what we do that's important and what we do that is a complete waste of time.

5. I challenge you to write a mission statement. This practice has changed my life for the better and I know for sure that it will have a positive impact on yours. See the back of the book for tips on how to write a mission statement.

Make It Counter: Aaron Nicholas

Aaron Nicholas, DDS, has been a practicing dentist for 30+ years in Burtonsville, MD. He is a serial entrepreneur with a keen interest in teaching, coaching and mentoring his fellow dentists. He is the founder of Monday Morning Dentistry, The Dental Assistant School of Maryland and The Smile Protection Dental Plan, as well as co-founder of the Kickstarter Dental Coaching Program. Additionally, he is one of the "Blackbelt" coaches with the Dental Success Institute. He has spoken about dental efficiencies and practice management both locally and internationally and has authored many instructional programs about these topics and conducted hands-on courses across the U.S.

Dr. Nicholas has been interviewed on numerous podcasts including, *The Dentalpreneur Podcast, The Relentless Dentist Podcast, Dentists, Implants and Worms and The Better Dentistry Podcast*, to name a few.

However, the activity of which Aaron is most proud is traveling each year with a humanitarian team that provides dental care to the poorest of the poor in the Dominican Republic. This is a passion that started in dental school and continues to this day.

While all of this sounds wonderful, Aaron feels that none of it would have been possible or worthwhile without the love and support of his wife Anahit and numerous friends and colleagues.

What are your top three habits that have supported your success over the years?

Hmm, top three habits…

First, EXERCISE!...It's good for what ails you!
If you had a bad day at work or school it helps to relieve the stress and get your mind off things for a while. When you're done, you're usually in a better place to go back and work on the situation. It also gives you space to calm down and see the situation differently. If everything else went wrong today, at least I got a good workout in. It helps develop self discipline. If you're going to accomplish anything you will need self discipline. Exercise can be a great springboard for that.

Second, PERSISTENCE

When I was younger I thought that some people were just gifted, or talented, or lucky, or...you name it. But I found that as I got to hear people's stories that there were very good reasons for their good fortune. Sure, sometimes luck plays a part but, I've also found that if I've been putting in the work I seem to get "luckier." I think we all want to believe in magic - that if we do the right things, what we want will magically happen. But, I think the truth is that if we really want something and are willing to sacrifice and not give up on it, we can have most anything we want. But it won't necessarily be easy, or feel magical. Sometimes we may even decide that what we have to do to get this coveted thing, just isn't worth it. And that's legit too! I've heard that 80% of success is persistence. That sounds about right. Someone also once said that 80% of success in life is just showing up. That sounds about right too. So many people don't, or won't, show up, put in the work and just take care of business. When we see someone who does, it stands out as exceptional. Really, in many ways, the bar for success is pretty low.

Third, ALWAYS BE MOVING FORWARD

I am unhappy and defeated when I'm not moving and I have no agenda; when I have no new projects or goals or when I have no new thoughts or ideas. Earlier on I was always trying to be successful, figuring that once I got there I would be happy and satisfied. So obviously, the object was to get there ASAP. So I could live in Nirvana. And at times I have hit all the goals I had set for myself. And it was NOT Nirvana. Instead, I felt lost and depressed. Yes, I know, there is a certain threshold of success one needs to feel secure. But once that is reached, humans need goals and aspirations to reach for.
Sometimes they will be in business, sometimes in our personal lives or sometimes in our spiritual lives. But we're either growing or dying. Physically, we have no choice. But in every other arena of life it's really up to us. I am happiest moving forward!

I am amazed at people who lose significant amounts of weight. You have lost roughly 100 pounds over the years. What have you learned about yourself during the process, and how has that improved your life?

I lost 100lbs while in my early 30s. I had been fat as a child and had lost weight and became an active teenager and college student. I then gained weight (286 at my heaviest) because I was depressed, lonely and isolated (all self induced) for quite a while. The decision to lose weight happened in an instant. Sure, I had been thinking I needed to lose a little weight for a while but, that's all it was, thoughts. Then, one day, as I heard myself talking to friends about the "great" vacation I had just returned from, what I heard was me describing doing nothing but eating and watching movies. In that moment it sounded like the most pathetic thing I had ever heard. I decided that I was much too young to go through the rest of my life like this. I couldn't do any of the things that I had enjoyed when lighter (playing tennis, ice hockey, running, basketball) and I couldn't remember the last time I had had a date. Actually, I could but, things were depressing enough without that too. So, I made the decision and it took 2 years. It started out with a bet with a friend. We each lost 40 lbs in 5 months. My friend wasn't interested in another round of weight loss, so I had to go it alone. I dieted. I exercised. Some weeks were better than others. But I knew that if I could lose the weight I could go back to doing the things I had enjoyed before. I also knew that I wanted to have someone special in my life and that wasn't going to happen with me being a hefty 286lbs!

I think this was the real key to my weight loss. I wasn't giving up something - I was getting something. I wasn't giving up food, I was getting my life back! It was just a matter of doing what I needed to do in order to have it. And persisting. This was probably the first time that I had done something that was really hard for me and for which I didn't have any natural gift. While I enjoyed playing sports, I was really bad almost all of them. I just liked to play. And I had always been a little heavy my whole life. So this victory was really me seeing that I could even do things that I didn't have any natural abilities for, if I put my mind to it.

What has been your greatest failure and what did you learn from it?

One of my greatest failures, actually there were two, was when I had two complete staffs of employees quit on me. It wasn't a wholesale walkout. But, little by little, they all quit. They were good people and good employees. I really liked some of them. And it was personal, at least to me. So, one day I literally sat in a chair and tried to think through the problem and solve my "staff retention" issue. And the only plausible answer is that I was the problem. After all, I was the only common denominator between the two staffs. See, I didn't have very good "people skills" back then. I certainly wasn't a natural leader or communicator. But I did have a very good friend who was a family therapist. So, going forward, each time I had a staff issue I would call him and discuss what happened and what I intended to do about it. Usually, he would give me an alternative viewpoint and many times suggested better ways of handling the situation. So little by little I started to become a better boss and better human.

My number one rule these days is that if everyone around me is screwing up and unreasonable, it's a pretty sure bet that I'm the problem. I need to look inward first and get my issues dealt with before talking to anyone. This rule saves me from needing to make a lot of apologies later on.

You travel once a year to under-developed countries to provide free dentistry. Part of the "Make It Count" mission is being other-people focused. How has doing this improved your mindset and your approach to life?

It used to be that travel was regarded as its own form of education. I think we need to re-embrace that idea. When you see how most of the rest of the world lives, it's hard not to be grateful for what we have in this country. We are safe. We have clean water. We don't have rampant diseases that kill multitudes of people. We have social programs for the needy. We have access to health care. (Yes, I know that these are available to different segments of the population to varying degrees but the fact remains that we have more of this than anywhere else on earth and we're still working on these issues.) When you see people without these things who are still happy and loving and giving, it's hard not to feel a little ashamed of what you take for granted. Seeing the rest of the world makes me truly grateful for what I have, makes me more human and, hopefully, keeps me humble. Knowing that, "but for an accident of birth" (whether you believe in accidents or not) our roles could have been reversed changes your perspective.

What is your favorite book and why?

Extreme Ownership, How the US Navy Seals Lead and Win
    by Leif Babin and Jocko Willink

I think I am drawn to their dedication to their family, their teammates, their duty and their country. It tells the story of how they worked in a bureaucracy, which many times had multiple agendas, and still stayed true to their values and beliefs. Normal for this situation was that everyone was grumbling, complaining and trying to get away with as much as possible. However, they took ownership of everything that was happening around them and completely changed the organization of which they were a part.

What are three non-negotiables that have led to both your personal and business success over the years?
Honesty
Integrity
Treat the next person as you would want to be treated

What piece of advice would you give someone coming fresh out of dental school, about the tools and tactics needed to be successful in the long run?

First, see #6 above. Remember, you're in this for the long haul
Check your ego at the door, keep an open mind. You'll learn a lot more a lot faster that way. Always have a coach or mentor.   Hang out with people you want to be like.
Don't go it alone

What do the words "Make It Count" mean to you?

None of us asked to be here. But now that we're here we have a couple of choices.

We can just look out for ourselves, our ease and our own

OR

We can make our lives count…
-to serve God and each other
-to make a difference in humankind
-to live a life beyond our own personal comforts
-to care for those less fortunate
-to use the gifts with which we've been blessed

CHAPTER 23

Make It Count

"Don't count the days; make the days count."

- Muhammad Ali

Why should you care?

Why even bother with trying to "Make It Count?"

Why should you need a book of principles to live your life by?

The quick answer for you is that you really don't have to care. You're not being forced to apply anything in this book to your life. I can't make you -- no one can make you do something you don't want to do. We all have choices in this journey, and your choice is to either go ALL in or sit in the back seat and just wait for things to happen. Either way, you're the one who controls whether things happen or not. But seeing that you've almost finished this book, I can only assume that the thirst for just one reason to live a more accomplished life is within you.

Let's have a look at the following storyline. Assuming you're 40 years old today, we'll fast forward another 40 years to the fine age of 80. Imagine you wake up one morning consumed with regret and fear and anxiety. These emotions aren't related to your age or health, but they consistently show up in your life because of your regret for not chasing the dreams of your youth. It's not that you never had any intentions for greatness in your life, you just never got around to pulling the trigger. You lived small -- concerned with the opinions of others and a fear that failure would define the legacy of your life. You lived outside of your bookends, focusing on the wrong principles. You feared taking massive action, not because of the success it would bring but because of what it would take to reach that success. Fear. This is the one topic that I haven't gotten too deeply into throughout this book. What scares us? Fear can be a paralyzing emotion that holds us back from our true potential. We not only avoid the uncomfortable chapters in our life, but when we are afraid, we tend to quickly turn the page in hopes that it will disappear. But what if we captured that fear, and used it for good instead? Embracing the "Make It Count" lifestyle is essentially conquering what we fear.

Over the years, I have learned that the harder I chase the ability to "Make It Count," the more I am able to overcome the things I am afraid of. My biggest fear has always been — and I hope that it will always be — not being a good enough dad for my kids. Not having my own dad around while growing up led to a very realistic fear as I got older. I was afraid that I would fall into his footsteps. I was afraid that I would become not only an alcoholic, but someone who was never present. But I came to understand that my path was completely within my control. I decided I would have to fight hard each day for all of the principles I knew and loved.

My present mentality is focused on being the best version of myself, out of fear for what the other version might look like. That fear forces me to wake up each day and do everything in my power to be better. If I let the fear win, then I am essentially letting myself off the hook for not pursuing excellence. My mentality is not about doing more so that my day is totally full. Peter Drucker said it best, "There is nothing so useless as doing efficiently that which should not be done at all." Instead, my mentality is about doing fewer things more *efficiently* so that I can enjoy what matters most to me. Without structure and a means to an end, we end up processing busy work all day long. When we find a passion, a purpose, and a reason to "Make It Count," our efficiency level jumps to a new starting point. We end up focusing on what is most meaningful in our day because that is where our priorities lay.

When we actually sit down and discuss all of the techniques in this book, we embrace that this lifestyle and journey is about *all of us*. We all deserve the chance to treat and respect each other on the same level. We are all going through difficult stuff, and that stuff needs to be addressed. Otherwise, the cascade effect of negative outcomes will take over. When we invest in this lifestyle, we are absolutely maximizing our ability to live each moment with purpose. And that purpose becomes helping those around us to realize that to "Make It Count" means to challenge ourselves in each situation to find the best outcome. When we are making the best of life, our least efficient actions disappear. We realize that fixating on options that are not beneficial to our future is a waste of our emotional and physical energy.

Any event, and I mean *any* event, from your past needs to be evaluated as a learning experience. The second you start to obsess over something that has already happened is the second when you stop living in the moment. Life will challenge you, without a doubt. Some challenges will be your fault, and others will be totally out of your control. All of them should be used as perspective for what you should do next. To stress over something from the past is to take away from the excellence of what you could be doing right now. This lifestyle is about helping those around you to see the greatness within themselves. Generally, the human mind finds itself in search of mediocrity. Mentally, we set out to do amazing things with a vision of a better version of ourselves. Then we start to hold back, we cut corners and fall into a world of excuses as to why we can't do or be something. We cheat our way out of greatness, and we fall into a world of being just average.

There's nothing wrong with being average, if that is your intent from the beginning. But if you were given the option to either live out your dream or settle for being average — I'm willing to bet that the majority of you would choose living out your dream.

Mediocrity happens, not because it's meant to be, but because we let it slip into our mainstream. But even if you pick any chapter in this book and apply only *that* chapter to your life, I guarantee you'll find yourself living a life above average.

Take the "Sunny and Cloudy" concept, for instance. This simple, yet profound, activity has helped so many people I have introduced it to. It opens us up to so much in our lives that we may not be showing enough gratitude for. And when all we can come up with is a cloudy, it still opens up our mindset to change. Ending the day by evaluating how that day went, with both the good and the bad, gives us the chance to determine whether or not we are "Making It Count." Ignore the process, and we get lost in the woods of what we are doing.

Every principle comes with the common understanding that life is about being "other people focused." When you understand that your vision, thoughts, and actions revolve around wanting the best for other people, then your life raises to another game changing level. Adding value, being humble, exercising, telling your story, and asking better questions will all help establish your foundation in this world. But what you are really doing is becoming a better human to help those around you express their own greatness.

This lifestyle is about finding a reason or a need, and taking the time to fulfill that need today rather than tomorrow. Watch the news, read the paper, or scroll through social media, and you will see dozens of stories about people whose journeys have ended. Some you may know, while others you don't. It seems we have become immune to the fragility of life, and we tend to think that certain things just couldn't happen to us. If you take anything away from this book, let it be that things *can and do* happen. You're not immortal, and **today** is your chance to make a difference.

What I *don't* want you to do is to read this book, put it down, and implement nothing into your journey. The key to change is not making a full overhaul of the system, but instead making small changes and implementing them until they become habits. When the principles within this book become habits, then you can continue to upgrade the system to find out what works best within your bookends.

One morning, you wake up not to the sound of your alarm, but to the energy of living life with purpose. You turn on the coffee pot and notice a card neatly propped up next to your favorite mug. You open the card to see a bright, rainbow colored birthday card from your grandkid that reads, *"Happy 80th Birthday!!!"* The emotions of gratitude, happiness, and joy flood your mind. Sticking to routine and habits, you sit down to write in your morning journal. This time it's not about the present, but instead about how you have crushed life over your 8 decades. Instead of fear and regret, your mind runs deep with the pride of knowing that you woke up each and every day ready to "Make It Count."

Your life has not been a constant struggle to climb, but instead a roller coaster ride in which you excelled through each rise and fall. You celebrated the peaks just as much as the valleys, because without constant progression, life is a flat line. You realized at a young age that in order to "Make It Count" and live out the vision of what you desired, you would have to always jump in and take massive action. Dreams and goals were a constant, but what took you to the next level was the ability to know that the fear of not living was stronger than the fear of holding back.

"Make It Count" is not a perfect plan for living the life you want. At the of the day, the decisions are entirely in your grasp. "Make It Count" simply gives you the fuel to go after your dreams, and to live a journey worth celebrating once you reach that 80th birthday. You owe that to yourself and to those you love -- to live a life that you can be proud of, in every respect.

So my last question to you is, "How will you start your **Make It Count** journey?"

Make It Count Foundations

1. Perspective is the gift that keeps giving. When we understand the impact of perspective, we see each and every moment as a chance to grow.

2. We all have stories, failures, moments of growth, and events that happen all the time in our lives. No one's story is more important than the next, but all of our stories can grow upon each other exponentially. Share your story as a chance to inspire, not because you think you're better than anyone else.

3. To "Make It Count" is to assess a desire or need to make something in your life and the lives those around you better.

4. "Make It Count" is not about perfection because perfection doesn't exist. Instead, it is about taking one or more principles from this book and implementing them into your lifestyle. Simple strategies produce enormous results. When the strategy is difficult, we have trouble holding onto consistency. When possibly all we have to do is smile a little more, then our impact not only multiplies but becomes a habit we can be proud of.

5. Principles, metrics, paradigms -- no rules are cookie cutter, made to fit everyone's life. Any self-improvement, self-development, or success endeavour you come across should be taken with a grain of salt. Not everything will fit perfectly into your life, nor should it. If you force a principle and it doesn't feel right, then you will associate with that principle in a negative way. You will consistently work to avoid it. Take note from everything you learn and see what fits into your world. The key is to find some avenue to be better daily, to understand that time is limited, and most importantly to "Make It Count!"

Make It Counter – Lorraine Tegeris

Lorraine's personal development journey started when she found the book *Illusions* by Richard Bach on her mom's bookshelf when she was 14 years old. Since then, she has read thousands of books and attended countless workshops. She earned her BS degree in Chemistry from MIT with a minor in Psychology and, after college, worked for 11 years as Director of Quality Assurance for Savanet, a pharmaceutical testing firm. She has also worked as a Trainer with Robbins Research International (RRI) for over 20 years, and is currently a Master Trainer with RRI. Lorraine's main work focus now is as Chief of Content Development for Trusum Visions, an online personal growth company. Lorraine and her husband, John, have been together for 27 years; she is proud mom to 3 kids, 1 grandchild, and 2 puppies.

What one thing has had the greatest impact on your life?

My love of reading! Reading for pleasure, reading for growth, reading for enlightenment, reading for learning, reading for any reason! I love the idea that we're all standing on the shoulders of the giants who have come before us. Reading is one way to make other people's wisdom your own, and to move forward from there.

You have worked with Tony Robbins for a long time now. How do you think working with Tony has helped you personally?

The biggest lesson I've learned from Tony Robbins is about taking 100% responsibility for your experience of life; that your quality of life is dependent on the meanings that you give to your experiences. You can't always control what happens to you in life, but you can always control how you respond and what you make it mean.

If you had a billboard to fill with a favorite quote or a favorite saying what would it say?

Wow, that's a tough one! I'm a big fan of the quote by Abraham Lincoln that says, "Whatever you are, be a good one." That quote reminds me to do my best and be my best no matter what I'm doing, no matter what's going on. Whether it's something I've deliberately chosen, or something life has handed me, I own it and show up to the best of my ability.

You have worked with my daughter for close to two years now as her soccer coach and I have noticed that the kids love the visualization exercises you have presented to them over time. Why do you think exercises like visualization are important for success?

Ah, great question! I honestly believe that visualization is one of the most important tools in everyone's toolbox. It can be done anywhere, at anytime to "practice" performance of any kind, sports or otherwise. Because the mind can't tell the difference between something that actually happens and something that's vividly imagined (ever been scared by a dream!), visualization is a great way to get "perfect" practice over and over.

Your professional career has been centered around personal development and self improvement. What piece of advice would you give a younger version of yourself knowing the information you know now?

Don't be afraid. Everything will be alright in the end, and if it's not alright yet, it's not the end.

Do you believe in motivation? Some professionals within the personal development world have been shifting to finding a deeper meaning than motivation as motivation never seems to be there when you need it. What would you tell someone looking to be motivated?

To me, motivation is really about purpose, it's about your "why." Why do you want to do whatever it is you need motivation for? Why is it a "must" that you do this, and do it now? What are all the rewards that you'll gain by doing it, and what pain will you feel if you don't get yourself out there? The key is to get fully associated to your answers to those questions; motivation is driven by emotion.

What are your top three habits that are non-negotiable to your life? These are habits that you hold strong with and you have a deep purpose to always carrying them out.

The top three habits that come immediately to mind aren't habits of action, they're habits of attitude. The first and most important attitude habit I live by is Kindness; that's absolutely 100% non-negotiable. The second would be along the lines of never quit, never give up, just keep going. The third habit is a mix of action and attitude, it's to immediately look for a solution to any and every challenge that I face. I believe there's always a way.

What do the words "Make It Count" mean to you?

The first idea that comes to mind when I think "Make It Count" is touching someone's life for the better; having a positive impact on another person's moment, their day, their life. We're all on this planet together, let's Make It Count and work together for the good of everyone.

MAKE IT COUNT
POEMS

I am Powerful!!!! – Avery Oergel

Be a strong, powerful girl
Stand up to what **YOU THINK IS RIGHT!!!**
Have a spark of fire in your soul that takes away all fear

Fight till the end
DON'T stop until you have accomplished something
Step to boys and let them know **WHO YOU ARE!!!**

Whether you play sports, write, read, act or just do an everyday job
MAKE IT COUNT!!!

DON'T let anyone tell you that you are not good enough or that you can never do
something

Step forward and show them who's boss!!!

Be the next person that someone says I want to be like her

DON'T hold back from the world

Discover what you are made of

NOW GO BE POWERFUL!!!

Make It Count

Poolside – Chelsea Young

Sitting back looking at your life,
What do you see? What are you now?
What's next?

The difference between thinking of where it may go
and where it actually goes.
Thinking of your plan, your story
and how it will be told.

But everything seems so daunting.
One thing after another.
One year after the next.
Where does life all go?

Moments only last so long,
but memories will continuously be made.

How much happiness lies ahead?
How much heart break can one endure?
How much excitement is out there waiting?

Life can be very unexpected,
but only you control your happiness,
and all decisions to come.

So whatever your plan is,
whatever goals you set and
whatever you want your life story to be,
go after it.

Life isn't going to wait for you.
Life never stops.
Time is ticking, so starting living every moment
the way you perfectly imagined.

MAKE IT COUNT TOOLS

100th Birthday Talk

The key to this activity revolves around one important question: What type of life do you want to live? Odds are not great -- though getting better with advancements -- that you will live to 100. That is not the point of this activity though. The activity surrounds visualization. Racing competitively for close to 20 years in triathlon, visualization became not only helpful but necessary for my success. It helped me focus on the race, on what could go right, on what could go wrong, and on hopefully being ready for anything. Writing down your 100th birthday talk is a process of visualizing what you want your life to look like. There will be peaks and valleys, but if your foundation is strong, you will be able to conquest any direction life takes you. On this page, however long it takes you, write down your celebration list of what you were grateful for during your 100 years!!!

Non-negotiables List

Write out your top 10 non-negotiables list. This list will become the foundation of your "Make It Count" journey. The key is to take your time with your answers. If you rush through this and don't fully identify with the list, then you're just making a list to make a list. This assignment is not graded by any person, but by how you live your life. The list means nothing to anyone, as far as lists go, but it will have a huge impact on how you conduct yourself and how you interact with others. Your non-negotiables may look very similar to your mission statement, and that is okay. We can make decisions with ease and confidence once we have identified what's important.

1. _____
2. _____
3. _____
4. _____
5. _____
6. _____
7. _____
8. _____
9. _____
10. _____

Perfect Day

If we don't make time for what's important, then life will decide what's important for you. Everything starts with an incredible, consistent morning routine. When you structure your time in the morning, you structure your time for the rest of your day. Having a routine makes decisions easier as you have less stress in the decisions that need to be made. When we own the day, we own our time! Writing out your perfect day helps you to maximize your time, and maximizing your time helps you to "**Make It Count!**"

Here is an example of my perfect day:

4:00 AM - Wake - No snooze button because when you hit snooze, you're telling yourself that your goals are not important.

4:00-6:15 AM - Coffee, let dog out, read for 30 minutes and write for the rest of the time.

6:15-7:15 AM - Crush breakfast, drive to work getting ready to make people feel better. Optimize drive time listening to book or favorite podcast. Always be learning!

7:15 - 11:00 AM - Blessed with chance to help people get out of pain and chase their goals.

11:00 - 1:00 PM - Exercise as most important habit we can create in our day.

1:00 - 1:30 PM - Lunch for recovery of the mind and body.

1:30 - 3:30 PM - Return emails, calls, social media, more writing and house to do list.

3:30 - 8:00 PM - Family, family, family, family, family, family - most important part of my day as they fill me with anything and everything I need to Make It Count!

8:00 - 9:00 PM - Write out big goals for next day, gratitude journal, mobility work and then sleep.

Daily Gratitude

The chapter on "Sunny/Cloudy" details how we can work on gratitude in our life. Gratitude creates an environment that allows us to visualize the good that we have in times when life seems hard. Gratitude is also fuel for your day, and a way to maximize what you have or push you to achieve what you desire. Every morning and every evening, you can embark on gratitude writing. When we incorporate this into our daily habits, we are constantly aware of the good in our lives. My daily routine looks like the following, however you can create your own version that will work best for your schedule.

Morning

- Three things you are grateful for.
- Three big actionable goals for the day.
- Quote for the day.
- What would make today great?

Evening

- Three things that went well today.
- Three lessons learned from the day.
- Three people I had an impact on.
- First action plan for the next morning.
- Did I "Make It Count?"

Mission Statement

Your personal mission statement is the foundation of who you are. I chose a picture of my favorite place and I chose the values and metrics that mean the most to me. I read this every morning, as it hangs on the wall in my office. Done correctly and done with what matters the most to you, this activity will be extremely powerful for keeping you straight towards what's most important in your day.

Make It Count!!!
#1 focus is family so don't sacrifice anything for the gift you where given.
Seek to understand before judge
Exercise breads success
Drive inspiration and motivation into the lives of others
Spread optimism
Growth mindset trumps fixed mindset
Meditation clears the mind
Obstacle is the way
Grateful for the journey
Laugh often
Communication is the foundation of teamwork
Never stop learning
Follow complaints with positivity
Leave a legacy that inspires
Never go to bed angry
Work hard to make money in order to help others
Teach girls paradigms for success
Love unconditionally

Mission Statement:

Make It Count!!!
#1 focus is family so don't sacrifice anything for the gift you where given
Seek to understand before judge
Exercise breads success
Drive inspiration and motivation into the lives of others
Spread optimism
Growth mindset trumps fixed mindset
Meditation clears the mind
Obstacle is the way
Grateful for the journey
Laugh often
Communication is the foundation of teamwork
Never stop learning
Follow complaints with positivty
Leave a legacy that inspires
Never go to bed angry
Work hard to make money in order to help others
Teach girls paradigms of success
Love unconditionally